® Independent
Investigation
Method

Teacher
Manual

REVISED EDITION

7 Easy Steps
to Successful
RESEARCH

for Students in
Grades K-12

ACTIVE
LEARNING
Systems **LLC**

Cindy Nottage & Virginia Morse

Training for Research and Other Thinking Skills

P.O. Box 254 • Epping, New Hampshire 03042
Tel: (800) 644-5059   Fax: (603) 679-2611   E-mail: info@iimresearch.com
Web Site: www.iimresearch.com

Cindy Nottage, M.A. and Virginia Morse, M.A., Educational Consultants

Active Learning Systems offers professional training for teachers and administrators in student research skills, thinking skills, gifted and talented programming, curriculum compacting, and authentic assessment. Master teachers Cindy Nottage and Virginia Morse are the founders of Active Learning Systems and the developers of the Independent Investigation Method, a research process for students in grades K-12. They have experience in classroom teaching, special education, staff development, reading consultation, and gifted and talented program development and coordination.

Cindy and Virginia developed the Independent Investigation Method eighteen years ago for use in their own classes and introduced it to all grade levels at their schools where it was extensively tested and refined. Because of the popularity of "Double I.M.", Active Learning Systems now publishes IIM materials and provides training for educators internationally.

Design and production by Design Point Studio, Salisbury, N.H. 603-934-4082
Illustrations by Kerry Lott

IIM is a registered trademark of Active Learning Systems LLC

ISBN 978-1-57652-055-0

Notes from the Authors

All students can do research

In the revised edition of *IIM: Independent Investigation Method Teacher Manual*, we hold to this philosophy more strongly than ever. In the twenty-four years since we developed IIM, we have continued to see students from non-readers to the most academically gifted succeed with this model. IIM is a process that actively involves students in their own learning, empowers them to access information, and helps them to become independent, responsible, confident, excited researchers. This may take more time than some methods; however, students will learn not only the content in the curriculum but also a set of study skills. It is good for all students because it can be differentiated according to grade, skill, and academic ability needs.

In this manual there are two levels – Basic and Proficient. At the Basic Level, students learn the foundation skills of research that allow them to conduct independent research studies. The Proficient Level extends the progression of research skills for secondary school students who have experience with the foundation skills taught at the Basic Level of IIM. The same two strategies are used for teaching research skills at both levels: the Group IIM Process in which the whole class works together, and the Independent IIM Process in which students research individually. At both levels, the skills essential for success in the research process are taught in a progression according to the needs of the class. IIM is not a set of workpages that students must complete every time they do a research project. It is, instead, a set of skills that allows them to gather, analyze, and share information.

All students will learn that:
1. Research is a sequential process
2. Research is used to answer questions
3. There are many sources for information
4. They must cite their sources using a standard format for their bibliography
5. They need to put information in their own words
6. Information must be organized for use in a product
7. They should share what they have learned with an appropriate audience

Whether students are working at the Basic or Proficient Level of IIM, as a group or independently, they are learning lifelong skills which can be used throughout their schooling and into their careers.

Happy Researching!

Cindy &
Virginia

Using **IIM**: The Model

The Independent Investigation Method is a teaching model that guides students through the research process. Within this model, there are two skill levels: Basic and Proficient. Each level consists of a Group Process where the whole class studies one topic together and an Independent Process where students research topics individually or in small groups. The Group IIM Process at the Basic Level is appropriate for students K-8. Secondary teachers might prefer to introduce or review IIM using the Group IIM Process at the Proficient Level.

With the Independent IIM Process, your students will work on individual or small group studies. All students need to begin at the Basic Level where the foundation skills necessary for more advanced research are taught. The Proficient Level is for older students who have mastered basic research skills and are capable of applying the higher level skills required at this level.

Because IIM is really a continuum of skills, the process and progressions you choose should be based on your goals as well as your students' research experience, grade, and skill level. Use the following diagram to guide your choice as your students progress from beginning to advanced researchers. You will find more information in the introduction to each level and process to help you make choices for your class and unit.

IIM: Independent Investigation Method
Research Model

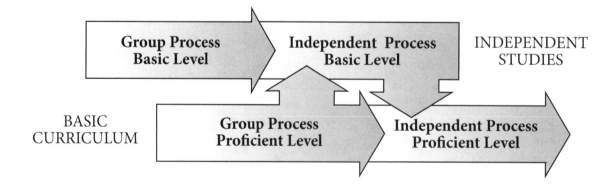

Using IIM®: The Manual

The *IIM: Independent Investigation Method Teacher Manual* will provide you with all the instructions and reproducible pages you need to teach the IIM model of research to students in Grades K-12.

Nine sections guide you through the process, lay out options for developing your curriculum, give you assessment suggestions, and provide supporting resources. Sections One-Three (Basic Level) and Sections Four-Six (Proficient Level) highlight the flow of the process. Here you will find detailed instructions on what you and your students will do during research, reproducible pages for designing and implementing your units, and sample research studies using the Independent Process. Section Seven contains forms to use in assessing the research process and its products. Section Eight includes teacher resource pages. Section Nine gives information about other Active Learning Systems materials and training.

The CD contains all the reproducible teacher, student, and assessment pages which you can customize to fit your unit and student skill levels. It is both PC and Mac compatible.

Acknowledgments

We are grateful to the many teachers throughout the world who have used IIM in their classrooms and given us feedback as we have modified and improved IIM to make it both teacher friendly and a valid research method. Special thanks go to the practicing professionals in the Sanborn and Winnisquam Regional School Districts with whom we have taught and collaborated for many years, and to administrators in districts nationwide who have provided training and materials to help their teachers succeed in teaching research. Because of all of you, our model has continued to grow and flourish in directions we could never have envisioned twenty-four years ago.

Special thanks go to:

Lyn Pudloski
for developing and testing the beginnings of the Proficient Level
of the Independent Process,

Debbie Parsons
for taking the process into many Canadian classrooms
and using it as the basis of the research for her Masters Thesis,

Jann Leppien and Ogden Morse
for giving us expert feedback on the Proficient Level,

Steve Kossakoski
for his knowledge and expertise in the field of educational technology,

Sally Reis and Joe Renzulli
for providing the fertile ground at Confratute
where we developed and shared IIM, our own TYPE III,

Hannah Howard
for taking our random ideas and putting them into a sequential,
user-friendly, exciting format,

and finally,

our families
for supporting us with their patience, understanding,
and feedback during this lengthy process.

Table of Contents

SECTION ONE
IIM Basic Level "How To" 1

    Group IIM Process Overview 3
    Group IIM Process 7 Steps 5
    Independent IIM Process Overview 13
    Independent IIM Process 7 Steps 15

SECTION TWO
IIM Basic Level Reproducible Teacher & Student Workpages 23

    Teacher Workpages Overview 25
    IIM Unit Plan 27
    Group IIM Process Chart Headings & Icons 33
    Independent IIM Process Student Workpages 35

SECTION THREE
Basic Level Sample Research Study 73

    Dinosaur Unit Plan 74
    Student Booklet 79

SECTION FOUR
IIM Proficient Level "How To" 99

    Group IIM Process Overview 101
    Group IIM Process 7 Steps 103
    Independent IIM Process Overview 111
    Independent IIM Process 7 Steps 113

SECTION FIVE
IIM Proficient Level Reproducible Teacher & Student Workpages 121

    Teacher Workpages Overview...123
    IIM Unit Plan 125
    Group Proficient MI Product/Presentation 131
    Student Workpages 133

SECTION SIX
IIM Proficient Level Sample Research Study 157

    Civil War Unit 158
    Student Booklet 163

Table of Contents *(continued)*

SECTION SEVEN

IIM Assessment **187**

IIM Assessment Forms 189
Samples of the Forms 203

SECTION EIGHT

Teacher Resources **213**

Teaching & Thinking Skills Models 215
Enrichment TRIAD Model 216
Research Strategies 217
Skills Often Used in Research 218
Glossary 219
Bibliography...221

What's Up with Active Learning Systems

Active Learning Systems Training 225
Posters 226
A Mini-Lesson Using Good Question Cubes 227
The Parent Guide to Raising Researchers 228

SECTION ONE

IIM - Basic Level "How To"

The Basic Level of the Independent Investigation Method has been developed to teach the foundation skills that prepare students for advanced research. A complete sequence and vocabulary are part of the process. Students learn key skills at each of the 7 steps whether they are engaged in the Group or the Independent Process.

The plans for you to follow for both the Group IIM Process and Independent IIM Process are found on the pages for the 7 steps . Each one includes:

 Teacher Steps = what you should do at each of the seven steps,

 Student Steps = student behaviors,

 Teacher Tips = words of wisdom from the many teachers who have worked with IIM, and

 CD Tips = notes for teachers using the IIM Companion CD

CONTENTS - SECTION ONE

Group IIM Process Overview 3
Group IIM Process 7 Steps. 5
Independent IIM Process Overview 13
Independent IIM Process 7 Steps 15

Basic Level

Group IIM Process
(A Whole-Class Study)

OVERVIEW

The Basic Level of the Group IIM Process is a whole-class study used to introduce IIM at any grade level. This process may be used with any curriculum unit, and may serve as the class study of a whole unit. If, however, your goal is to have students research independently, begin with the Group IIM Process to model the 7 steps using a topic from the class unit before students begin researching their individual topics.

At this level, the class as a whole researches the same topic following the 7 steps. Students do not work independently; no individual student booklets are used. You will present 3-4 resources of different types (book, text book, video, speaker…) for the class to use together, and record information from these sources on chart paper. The headings for these charts may be done by drawing freehand, by tracing from an overhead projection, or by enlarging Sec. 2: p. 30-35 and attaching them to the chart paper. After research has been completed, the class will organize the notefacts which are then used to develop class or individual products. Additional resources and activities not used in the research process may broaden the unit of study.

Chart paper headings and IIM icons can be printed out from the IIM Companion CD.

SYNOPSIS
Basic Level – Group IIM Process

STEP 1 Topic

After introducing the class topic through immersion activities, the teacher works with the class to develop a concept map on chart paper, focusing on what students already know and what they want to learn.

STEP 2 Goal Setting

The teacher and students formulate goal setting questions on a class chart.

STEP 3 Research

The teacher presents resources and records notefacts on chart paper from each source.

STEP 4 Organizing

The students organize all notefacts in categories on chart paper.

STEP 5 Goal Evaluation

The teacher checks skills and knowledge acquisition.

STEP 6 Product

The students develop whole class, small group, or individual products that share new knowledge.

STEP 7 Presentation

The students present products to an appropriate audience.

Basic Level Group IIM Process
STEP 1-Topic

Teacher Steps

The teacher will:

a. Choose unit of study from regular curriculum

b. Fill out all sections of *IIM Unit Plan* (Sec. 2: p. 27-32) for group study

c. Choose no more than 3-4 resources for class research

d. Immerse students in unit topic using books, interest centers, bulletin boards, posters, experiments, models, filmstrips, videos, speakers, field trips…

e. Introduce students to process by showing IIM vocabulary and steps

f. Work with class to develop enlarged concept map on chart paper containing categories, prior knowledge, and questions

g. Enlarge *Glossary of the Study* heading (Sec. 2: p.33) to prepare a vocabulary/spelling chart to record key words

Student Steps

The students will:

a. Participate in immersion activities you choose which introduce topic

b. Contribute prior knowledge and questions to develop class concept map

c. Identify and learn key vocabulary/spelling words

Teacher Tips

- Grade levels can divide a unit into subtopics for each class to research (plants: trees, flowers, vegetables). The presentation can then be teaching other classes in the grade level about each subtopic.

- On the concept map, accept all information students offer. Any misinformation can be used later as a learning tool.

- You may want to allow students to add more details to the concept map with markers or strips of paper until you begin Step 3.

- Use the *Teacher Reflection Journal* (Sec 7: p. 190) to record key events in the study. Next year keep the good strategies; modify those that didn't go well.

- Use Sec 7: p.197 to assess your class throughout the study.

- You can design and save your unit plan electronically for easy retrieval and modifications using the IIM Companion CD.

- The *Glossary of the Study* chart heading can be printed out.

Basic Level Group IIM Process
STEP 2-Goal Setting

Teacher Steps

The teacher will:

a. Use Teacher Essential Questions from *IIM Unit Plan* (Sec 2: p.27) to guide goal setting session

b. Help students formulate good questions by listing teacher and class questions on chart paper to be posted throughout unit

c. Explain that additional goals include using 3-4 sources and learning key vocabulary and spelling words

Student Steps

The students will:

a. Work with you to formulate good questions

Teacher Tips

- Good questions are open-ended questions that will lead the class into research.
- Limit the number of open-ended questions so that research is not too generalized.
- A class chart is a good way to record new vocabulary words.
- Begin your assessment of the process by posting class goals for number and types of resources, amount of notefacts and vocabulary as well as goal setting questions.

Basic Level Group IIM Process
STEP 3-Research

Teacher Steps

The teacher will:

a. Enlarge *Notefacts* heading (Sec. 2: p. 34) to prepare chart paper for each resource

b. Refer to p. 49 for information about the notefact process

c. Teach concept of plagiarism

d. For each class resource, write appropriate bibliographic information on *Notefacts* chart paper

e. Focus students on finding answers to goal setting questions using class resources

f. Present one resource at a time

g. Record class notefacts from that source on *Notefacts* chart paper

h. Model paraphrasing for short, meaningful notefacts

i. Record each source number in all magnifying glasses on corresponding *Notefacts* charts

j. Repeat steps d.- i. with each source

k. Keep completed *Notefacts* charts posted in room

l. Continue to record key glossary words

Student Steps

The students will:

a. Identify notefacts from resource materials for you to record on *Notefacts* chart paper

b. Continue to identify and learn key vocabulary/spelling words

Teacher Tips

• Even though students may read about the topic individually, they will not be researching independently. They will be working as a group with classroom resources.

• Students will find information by having you read to them, watching a video or TV program together, conducting experiments, listening to a speaker …

• In a preschool class, you might want to record notefacts on a color-coded concept map.

• Primary teachers may use sentence strip paper for notefacts and organize them using the sentence strip chart holder.

• With older students, give each a common reading piece to underline/highlight key information that will then be recorded as class notefacts.

• Use a section from the text book as a common reading selection. This can be a homework assignment.

⊙ The *Notefacts* chart headings can be printed out.

Basic Level Group IIM Process
STEP 4-Organizing

Teacher Steps

The teacher will:

a. Enlarge *Organizing Notefacts* headings (Sec. 2: p. 35) to prepare chart paper for each category

b. Look for categories with students by rereading *Notefacts* charts and web information, focusing on goal setting questions

c. Write category names on *Organizing Notefacts* headings, attache headings to chart paper, and choose different color for each category

d. Cut notefacts into strips

e. Keep several notefacts to model category placement using facts that could fit into more than one category

f. Use sample notefacts to model category choice by coloring magnifying glass handle and gluing on chart

g. Pass notefact strips out to students, making sure that each child, pair, or group has at least one

h. Have students choose categories for placement of notefacts

i. Guide discussion of category choices, allowing students to explain each choice

j. Have students color in magnifying glass handles on notefact strips and glue notefacts to appropriate *Organizing Notefacts* chart

k. Continue until all notefacts are placed

l. Post all *Organizing Notefacts* charts for use in product and presentation steps

Student Steps

The students will:

a. Choose names and colors for categories

b. Choose category for individual notefacts

c. Defend category choice

d. Color in magnifying glass handle on notefact(s) to match category

e. Glue notefact(s) on *Organizing Notefacts* charts

Teacher Tips

- If students are non-readers, place all notefacts into categories as a class.

- You may want to pre-name categories for students or glue several notefacts with commonalties on each category sheet and have students decide on category names from the notefact attributes.

- With older students, after organizing is completed, you may want to begin the transition to Independent IIM by choosing one more class resource for small group research. Each group is assigned one of the posted categories and records more notefacts either on chart paper or *Notefact* pages (Sec. 2: p. 55) which are then added to the appropriate category and shared with the class.

- If available, use pieces of different colored butcher paper for each category.

- A legitimate category should have at least 3 notefacts in it.

- A miscellaneous category should have no more than 3 notefacts.

- ⊙ The *Organizing Notefacts* chart headings can be printed out.

Basic Level Group IIM Process
STEP 5-Goal Evaluation

Teacher Steps

The teacher will:

a. Check knowledge acquisition by having class give answers to goal setting questions

b. Use other ways of evaluating if appropriate: spelling/vocabulary test, chapter/unit test, small group discussion, individual conferences...

Student Steps

The students will:

a. Participate in evaluation activity(s)

b. Find additional notefacts if necessary

Teacher Tips

• Be sure that what you evaluate matches your unit plan objectives.

> **Teacher Example:**
>
> OBJECTIVE: Children will know the meaning of vocabulary words pertaining to the topic.
>
> EVALUATION: Students will label a diagram.

• If key goal setting questions are not answered during research, you might bring in an additional resource, or have students do individual research to find answers. This could be a good way to give more capable students a challenge.

• Some goal setting questions may not be answerable. This becomes part of the learning process.

• Assess vocabulary development by using words from *Glossary of the Study* in writing summary paragraphs.

Basic Level Group IIM Process
STEP 6-Product

Teacher Steps

The teacher will:

a. Decide how class can share knowledge gained by making group or individual products: book, play, bulletin board, poster, song, mural, dance, reenactment, graph, timeline …

b. Develop criteria for quality product

Student Steps

The students will:

a. Work with teacher to identify criteria for quality product

b. Develop class/small group/individual product

Teacher Tips

- Show samples of quality products for use in setting criteria for product development on a class chart, rubric…
- Teach students key skills to develop a quality product.
- Use category sheets as the basis for paragraph development, formal outlining, and descriptive writing.
- Assigning each student the same product type still allows students to display differences in knowledge acquisition, ability level, and learning style.
- For cooperatively produced products, you might give a group grade or grade each child's part individually.
- Design a product rubric using one of the Assessment Forms in Section 7.
- Rubrics can be customized on the CD.

Basic Level Group IIM Process
STEP 7-Presentation

Teacher Steps

The teacher will:

a. Choose appropriate audience(s) for product

b. Work with students to develop targeted presentation skills

Student Steps

The students will:

a. Display targeted skills when presenting product to audience

b. Share information gathered

Teacher Tips

- Student fact books can be used in the library as resources for other classes.
- Post the criteria for a quality presentation to ensure success.
- Presenting to younger classes is an effective way to share information.
- Practice with presentation equipment to help students develop self-confidence and poise in front of an audience.

Basic Level

Independent IIM Process

OVERVIEW

The primary purpose of the Independent IIM Process at the Basic Level is to teach students to research individual or small group topics. They will apply independently the foundatioon skills they learned in a whole class study using the Group Process at the Basic Level. These include key skills at each of the 7 steps starting with a topic, gathering and organizing facts, and sharing them through a creative product and possibly a report. More advanced pages will challenge older students as they continue to use the Basic Level.

In developing your research unit at the Basic Level, use the *IIM Unit Plan* (Sec. 2: p. 27-32) to identify academic, study skills, and assessment objectives and activities for your class. Here is the place to use state/local standards that will form the foundation of your unit. You might want to choose a teacher topic from the class unit so you can model the 7 steps and teach skills lessons for key objectives. In the Teacher/Student Steps, we have referenced the standard student pages from Section Two. When you assemble student booklets, make your choices at each step according to student skills, age level, and the nature of the study. Section Three shows a sample study at the Basic Level to help you understand how the Student Workpages are used.

Unit Plans, Student Workpages, and Assessment Forms can be designed and customized on the IIM Companion CD. The CD can also be used effectively for model lessons with a SmartBoard or another projection device.

SYNOPSIS
Basic Level – Independent IIM Process

STEP 1 Topic

Students web prior knowledge and questions on a concept map for their independent topic assigned or chosen from the class unit of study.

STEP 2 Goal Setting

The teacher helps students set goals for their research studies.

STEP 3 Research

Students use a variety of resource types to gather and record information using notefacts.

STEP 4 Organizing

Students organize notefacts by categories.

STEP 5 Goal Evaluation

Students demonstrate knowledge acquisition and skills development by completing teacher-chosen activity(s).

STEP 6 Product

Students create product(s) to show what they have learned during their research studies.

STEP 7 Presentation

Students present product(s) to an appropriate audience.

Basic Level Independent IIM Process
STEP 1-Topic

Teacher Steps

The teacher will:

a. Choose unit of study from regular curriculum

b. Fill out all sections of *IIM Unit Plan* (Sec. 2: p. 27-32)

c. Choose and copy pages for student booklets

d. Begin unit with class immersion activities

e. Introduce students to process by showing IIM vocabulary and steps

f. Work with students to make concept map of unit topic on chart paper, SmartBoard, or overhead

g. Brainstorm list of possible independent topics with class

h. Assign or help students choose topics

i. Have students read selection about their topics

j. Hand out introductory pages of student booklets (Sec. 2: p. 39-41) and guide students in recording information

k. Help students complete individual concept map with prior knowledge and questions (Sec. 2: p. 44)

l. Encourage students to find new vocabulary words key to their study and record on *Glossary of the Study* page (Sec. 2: p. 45)

Student Steps

The students will:

a. Work with teacher to develop class concept map and list of possible topics

b. Choose or be assigned topic of study

c. Record information on introductory pages of student booklet

d. Read selection about topic and web ideas on individual concept map

e. Begin to develop a key vocabulary/spelling words list

Teacher Tips

- Choose a unit from your grade level curriculum that is broad and allows each student to research a simple, concrete topic. See Section Three for sample unit plan.

- *Decision Making for Research Topic* (Sec. 2: p. 43) uses Talents Unlimited vocabulary (Sec. 8: p. 215). There are many other successful ways for students to choose their topics.

- Use a letter to inform parents of their child's topic and research date goals as well as how they can give support.

- Older students should use Sec. 2: p. 42 as their introductory page instead of Sec. 2: p. 40-41.

- Use your CD to design your new unit or modify one you have previously used.

- Print out collated student booklets after customizing selected pages.

Basic Level Independent IIM Process
STEP 2-Goal Setting

Teacher Steps

The teacher will:

a. Assign minimum number of resources, notefacts, and new key vocabulary/spelling words (Sec. 2: p. 46)

b. Identify required resource types

c. Work with students on setting individual notefact goal

d. Help students develop good questioning skills

e. Check each student's goal setting for purposeful questions

Student Steps

The students will:

a. Set goals for notefacts, resources, and new key words

b. Develop questions to direct research

Teacher Tips

- Fill in any information that will be the same for all students before copying the goal setting page.

- You may choose to add teacher questions to accomplish your unit goals.

- The class notefact goal should be attainable by all students. The individual notefact goal should be based on the student's ability level and prior research experience.

- If your students are ready to write a thesis statement or ask questions using Blooms Taxonomy, use Sec. 2: p. 47 or 48 for the goal setting page.

- ⊙ *Goal Setting* pages can be customized to reflect your unit goals.

Basic Level Independent IIM Process
STEP 3-Research

Teacher Steps

The teacher will:

a. Collect variety of resources for class library
b. Introduce many different types of resources
c. Explain concept of plagiarism
d. Teach students how to take notefacts using information on *Steps to Taking Notefacts* (Sec. 2: p. 49)
e. Demonstrate correct format for notefacts and bibliography (Sec. 2: p. 50-54)

Student Steps

The students will:

a. Learn to find and use variety of resources
b. Choose appropriate resources for topic
c. Conduct research by writing notefacts from resources following *Steps to Taking Notefacts*
d. Use correct format for bibliography (Sec. 2: p. 50-51)
e. Add to their glossary of new key vocabulary/spelling words (Sec. 2: p. 45)

Teacher Tips

- A classroom collection of resources is a must. Ask the school and town librarians to gather resources for you. Be sure to have a sign-out procedure for your room. It is important to include reference and fiction books, charts, posters, film strips, videos, web sites, artifacts, a listing of people and/or places to go to for information...

- Field trips and/or speakers are excellent sources of information. Students should be prepared to take notefacts to record pertinent information.

- Be sure to check each student's notefacts for correct form when s/he has finished between 3-5 notefacts. You will be able to nip copying in the bud at this stage.

- Other ways to prevent copying are: use a marker ("time saver") to cross out unnecessary words on student notefacts; vary the resources; vary the product; display a plagiarism sign...

- Enhance the IIM process and reinforce skills by tying into other academics: correct letter writing format, index and dictionary skills, graph interpretation, map reading, accessing electronic information, email interviews...

- Older students should develop the habit of writing the page number beside each notefact that comes from a text source.

- In a some units, teachers assign categories and students take notefacts using *Writing Organized Notefacts* (Sec. 2: p. 58-60) or *Notefact Grid* (Sec. 2: p. 61).

- Sec. 2: p. 55-57 use the standard notefact format but have narrower lines for older students.

- ⊙ You can select the categories/questions before printing out the *Notefact Grid*.

Basic Level Independent IIM Process
STEP 4-Organizing

Teacher Steps	*The teacher will:* a. Review concept of categories b. Introduce and have students follow *Steps to Organizing* (Sec. 2: p. 62) c. Help students identify individual notefact categories
Student Steps	*The students will:* a. Follow *Steps to Organizing* b. Write all source numbers of duplicate notefacts on one strip; throw duplicates away c. Identify areas that need more information, and go back to Step 3 for additional notefacts
Teacher Tips	• Honor student learning styles at this step. Some may be able to color-code notefacts before they cut them; others may need to manipulate notefacts before choosing categories and coloring. • Allow students to place notefacts in their own categories as long as they can justify the placement. • Don't allow more than 3 notefacts in the miscellaneous category. Students can usually find a new category or place the extras into existing categories. • Loose notefacts may be stored in an envelope. • Teachers have developed a variety of ways to have students identify their own notefacts: run a colored marker stripe down the back of the notefact pages (one color per student); put their initials on each notefact... • Have students sequence their notefacts before gluing or number them after gluing for better paragraph and report writing.

Basic Level Independent IIM Process
STEP 5-Goal Evaluation

Teacher Steps

The teacher will:

a. Review process assessment goals set in unit plan

b. Check knowledge acquisition with test, conference, small group discussion...

c. Guide students in evaluating goals set in Step 2 and in setting goals for future research (Sec. 2: p. 64)

Student Steps

The students will:

a. Demonstrate depth of knowledge acquisition by completing teacher chosen activity

b. Evaluate goals set in Step 2

c. Set goals for future research

Teacher Tips

- Teachers have found many creative ways of using this step to test knowledge acquisition: spelling/vocabulary tests, chapter/unit tests, small group discussions, individual conferences.... Individual conferencing is very rewarding but takes a great deal of time. Therefore, you may want to:

  a. Have students write 5 broad questions and answer them in their classroom presentation

  b. Have the whole class formulate general questions that each student will answer from his/her own research

  c. Group students with similar topics and have them share their questions and answers

- Any of the Student Workpages may be used for an individual conference, group conference, written evaluation, or to guide a group presentation.

- When writing a thesis statement, students should use Sec. 2: p. 65 for goal evaluation.

- Choose appropriate forms from Section 7: Assessment.

- Assessment forms may be customized on the CD.

Basic Level Independent IIM Process
STEP 6-Product

Teacher Steps

The teacher will:

a. Assign product type or have students use *Choosing a Product* (Sec. 2: p. 66) to guide product choices

b. Develop with class or assign criteria for quality product type(s)

c. Help students write plan for product (Sec. 2: p. 67)

d. Evaluate student products

Student Steps

The students will:

a. Choose or be assigned product type

b. Complete plan and create product showing what has been learned using product criteria

c. Add information to *IIM Product Tally* (Sec. 2: p. 68)

Teacher Tips

- You may assign the same type of product to every student or have each one choose his/her own. Encourage students to try different types of products with different units.

- Students may work as a class, in small groups, or individually to create a class product.

- Keep a record of products students have created to encourage them to expand to different product types.

- Develop a photo file of products for ideas and to use as exemplars and benchmarks for quality criteria.

- Before the product is started, develop criteria for quality products with the students or give them the quality criteria goals.

- Use Assessment Forms from Section 7 to record criteria for products.

- Keep criteria posted to guide quality work.

- Send criteria home with students for at-home products.

- ⊙ Assessment Forms may be customized to evaluate your unit goals.

Basic Level Independent IIM Process
STEP 7-Presentation

Teacher Steps

The teacher will:

a. Develop with class or assign criteria for quality presentations

b. Help students develop good presentation techniques using *My Presentation* (Sec. 2: p. 69)

c. Find appropriate audience(s) for product presentations

d. Evaluate student presentations

Student Steps

The students will:

a. Prepare for presentation using presentation criteria

b. Present product to audience

Teacher Tips

- Students need a chance to present their information to an audience of their peers, other classes, their parents…

- Be careful to limit the individual presentation time and the number per session.

- You might want to have a product fair where large groups can view the students' products. To encourage audience interaction, students should display questions that they can answer from their research. (Sec. 2: p. 71)

- If a written report has been a product, reading the report should not be part of the presentation.

- One class's presentation may be the way another class learns about a topic.

- In any classroom, the student researcher is the expert on his/her topic and learns about other topics from peer "experts".

- You should assess in some way what students have learned from other students' presentations.

- *Fact Gathering from Presentations* (Sec. 2: p. 70) allows students to record key information from other students' research. This can then be used as a study guide or in answering test questions.

- ⊙ Categories for *Fact Gathering from Presentations* may be recorded before students use this page.

- ⊙ Customized *Assessment Forms* are powerful tools for quality presentations.

SECTION TWO

IIM - Basic Level
Reproducible Teacher and
Student Workpages

These reproducible pages will provide you with the tools to develop and carry out your IIM units at the Basic Level. Use the *IIM Unit Plan* to identify goals and objectives, choose resources, design assessment tools, and develop skills lessons. The chart headings and icons you will need to implement a Group IIM are included. The Student Workpages give your students the structure to complete an individual or small group research study using the Independent IIM Process at the Basic Level. The overview of each part of Section Two gives additional information about the use of these pages.

The IIM Companion CD allows Teacher and Student Workpages to be edited.

CONTENTS - SECTION TWO

Teacher Workpages Overview 25
IIM Unit Plan 27
Group IIM Process Chart Heading and Icons 33
Student Workpages Overview 35
Independent IIM Process Student Workpages 37

Basic Level

IIM Teacher Workpages

OVERVIEW

These reproducible Teacher Workpages have been developed to aid you in unit and skills lesson planning, and in implementing the Group IIM Process at the Basic Level.

The *IIM Unit Plan* pages are an efficient way of developing, recording, and carrying out the learning objectives you have for your students for either the Group or Independent IIM Process. Use your state/local standards to identify academic and study skills objectives for the unit (p. 27). From these, list "How to" skills that need direct teaching lessons and record those lesson plans on p. 10. Tie your assessment plans (p. 29) to your objectives, and keep a record of key resources needed and used on p. 28. *The 7 Steps* (p. 30-31) serves as a flow chart of the total unit.

Also included in the Teacher Workpages are headings and icons (p. 33-36) to help you in implementing the Group IIM Process. These may be copied to use on chart paper.

The *IIM Unit Plan*, Assessment Forms and selected Student Workpages can be customized, saved, and printed out using the IIM Companion CD.

Objectives, Skills, & Standards
IIM Unit Plan

Curriculum Unit: _____ Class: _____

Dates: _____ Time: _____

Process Used (circle): *Basic Group* *Basic Independent* *Proficient Group* *Proficient Independent*

Academic and Study Skills Objectives:
Students will:

_____

_____

_____

_____

_____

_____

_____

_____

Teacher Essential Question(s):

_____

_____

_____

_____

_____

"How To" Skills:
Teach students "How to":

_____

_____

_____

_____

_____

Standards Addressed:

_____

_____

_____

_____

Resources
IIM Unit Plan

Curriculum Unit: _____

List the resources you will use during the unit. Be sure to include some that are appropriate for the diverse learning needs and styles within your classroom.

Print: (book, computer, poster...)

_____
_____
_____
_____
_____
_____
_____

Non-Print: (field trip, video, experiment...)

_____
_____
_____
_____
_____
_____

People: (speaker, parent volunteer, other teacher...)

_____
_____
_____
_____
_____

Preparatory Activities/Materials:

Student Booklet Pages: _____

Transparencies: _____

Other: _____

Immersion Activities: _____

_____

_____

_____

Assessment
IIM Unit Plan

Curriculum Unit: _____

What *process skills* will you assess?   How?

What *products* will you assess?   How?

7 Steps
IIM Unit Plan

Curriculum Unit: _____

List what you will do for each step of the process. Include unit activities, assessment strategies, and skills lessons. Identify ways you will differentiate for the diverse learning needs and styles of your students.

STEP 1 Topic

STEP 2 Goal Setting

STEP 3 Research

7 Steps
IIM Unit Plan *(cont.)*

STEP 4 Organizing

STEP 5 Goal Evaluation

STEP 6 Product

STEP 7 Presentation

Teaching "How To" Skills
IIM Unit Plan

Use this page to plan mini-lessons to teach key skills during the IIM unit.

Curriculum Unit: _____

Step: _____   Skill: _____

Date: _____   Class/Time: _____

Objectives:

_____
_____
_____
_____
_____
_____

Materials:

_____
_____
_____
_____
_____
_____

Procedure:

_____
_____
_____
_____
_____
_____

Notes:

_____
_____
_____

STEP 1-3   Topic - Research

Glossary of the Study

To make *Glossary of the Study* chart heading for the Basic Level of the Group IIM Process, enlarge 125% onto 8 1/2" x 14" paper.

STEP 3   Research

Notefacts

Source

To make *Notefacts* chart heading for the Basic Level of the Group IIM Process, enlarge 125% onto 8½" x 14" paper.

STEP 4 Organizing

Organizing

Organizing Notefacts

Notes About

To make *Organizing Notefacts* chart heading for the Basic Level of the Group IIM Process, enlarge 125% onto 8 1/2" x 14" paper.

Use these icons in various ways—for group *Notefacts* chart paper, bulletin boards, displays...

Basic Level

IIM Student Workpages

OVERVIEW

These reproducible Student Workpages have been developed for the Independent Process to guide your students through the 7 steps of IIM at the Basic Level. It is important to remember that these pages are not a workbook; not all pages should or could be used for one study. There are many options for each step, and pages should be carefully chosen to correspond to the unit content, objectives, and academic level of your students. Referenced in the Teacher Steps and Student Steps in Section One are the standard pages for the student booklet. Other possible pages are described in the Teacher Tips for the step in which they would be used.

The IIM Companion CD may be used to customize the Student Workpages for student booklets or for use in model lessons. It also is an effective teaching tool using a SmartBoard or another electronic projection device.

IIM® Independent Investigation Method

Hi! I'm Agent

Agent

Name:

STUDENT BOOKLET
Basic Level

Basic
Workpages

By: _____

Grade: _____

Teacher: _____

Class IIM Unit

_____

My IIM Topic

_____

Date Started: _____

Date Finished: _____

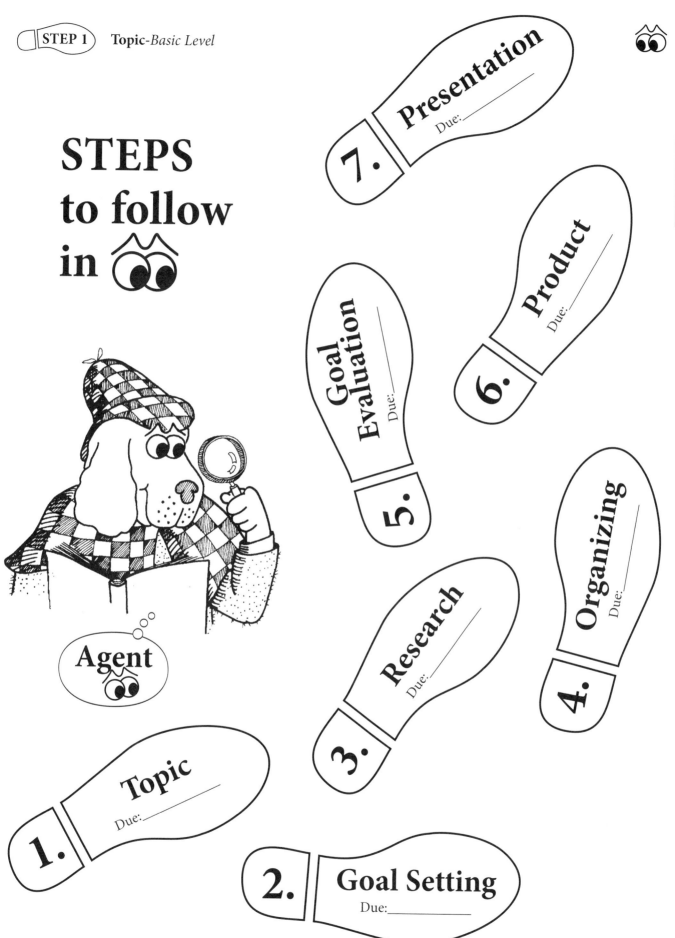

STEPS
to follow
in 👀

Agent

7. Presentation
Due:_____

Product
6. Due:_____

Goal
Evaluation
5. Due:_____

Organizing
4. Due:_____

Research
3. Due:_____

1. Topic
Due:_____

2. **Goal Setting**
Due:_____

STEPS to Follow in

Use this page to keep track of your progress during your research study. Check off steps as you complete them. Prepare your notebook for grading on the dates listed.

Name: _____

Class: _____

Class Topic: _____

My Topic: _____

Notebook Due Dates: _____   _____   _____   _____

		DUE	COMPLETED	GRADE
STEP 1	**Topic**			
	Concept Map:	_____	_____	_____
STEP 2	**Goal Setting**			
	Setting Research Goals:	_____	_____	_____
STEP 3	**Research**			
	Notefacts:	_____	_____	_____
	Bibliography:	_____	_____	_____
	Glossary:	_____	_____	_____
STEP 4	**Organizing**			
	Organizing Notefacts:	_____	_____	_____
STEP 5	**Goal Evaluation**			
	Evaluating Research Goals:	_____	_____	_____
STEP 6	**Product**			
	Report:	_____	_____	_____
	Other:	_____	_____	_____
STEP 7	**Presentation**	_____	_____	_____

Decision Making for Research Topic

1. State the PROBLEM:

_____

_____

_____

2. List some ALTERNATIVES:

_____

_____

_____

_____

3. List your CRITERIA:

_____

_____

_____

_____

4. Make your DECISION:

_____

_____

_____

5. Give your REASONS:

_____

_____

_____

_____

Basic Workpages

Concept Map

Basic Workpages

Web ideas about your *Topic* on the *Concept Map* using what you already know and questions about what you want to learn.

(My Topic)

Glossary of the Study

List the NEW words and their meanings that are key to the understanding of your topic.

Setting Research Goals

Notefact Goal: _____

Required Glossary Entries: _____

Required Number of Resources: _____

Required Resource Types: _____

_____

_____

_____

Resource Types

Book, magazine, Internet, TV show, letter, computer, interview, video/movie, poster, field trip...

My Topic: _____

Questions to Guide My Research
Teacher Question(s):

_____

_____

_____

_____

_____

My Questions:

_____

_____

_____

_____

_____

_____

Setting Research Goals *Using a Thesis Statement*

Notefact Goal: _____

Required Glossary Entries: _____

Required Number of Resources: _____

Required Resource Types: _____

_____

_____

Resource Types

Book, magazine, Internet, TV show, letter, computer, interview, video/movie, poster, field trip...

My Topic: _____

This *Thesis Statement* tells what I will try to prove from my research.

Sample a	Sample b
TOPIC: Causes of the Civil War	TOPIC: Pterodactyls
THESIS STATEMENT: The U.S. economy was the major cause of the Civil War.	THESIS STATEMENT: Pterodactyls are ancestors of birds.

My Thesis Statement: _____

_____

Teacher Question(s): _____

_____

_____

_____

My Questions: _____

_____

_____

_____

_____

Setting Research Goals *Using Bloom's Taxonomy*

Notefact Goal: _____

Required Glossary Entries: _____

Required Number of Resources: _____

Required Resource Types: _____

_____

_____

My Topic: _____

Teacher Question(s): _____

_____

_____

> **Resource Types**
>
> Book, magazine, Internet TV show, letter, computer, interview, video/movie, poster, field trip...

Write one question at each level of *Bloom's Taxonomy* to guide your research. **Remember!** A question can be a question ("What are the names of the planets?") or a questioning statement directing you to do something ("Name the planets.").

My Questions:

1. Knowledge: (find, list, name...) _____

_____

2. Comprehension: (define, review, identify...) _____

_____

3. Application: (apply, demonstrate, illustrate...) ___

_____

4. Analysis: (classify, compare, summarize...) _____

_____

5. Synthesis: (invent, predict, design, combine...) ___

_____

6. Evaluation: (judge, recommend, verify, evaluate...) _

_____

Steps to Taking Notefacts

These are directions to help you take **notefacts** for your IIM using the *Notefacts* pages. If you follow these steps, you will be on the way to becoming a good researcher.

1. Each resource you use will have its own number. Write that number in the large magnifying glass and on all the small magnifying glasses on your *Notefacts* pages.

2. Record required information for your bibliography on the solid lines.

3. Now you're ready to take-**notefacts**. Agent IIM calls them **notefacts** because they are short (notes) and true (facts).

4. **Notefacts** should be:

   - Written in your own words

   - Short but complete enough to make sense

   - Related to your goal setting questions

   - Written between the dotted lines — one **notefact** per space

   - Documented by page number

> *Don't be a plagiarist by stealing other authors' words*

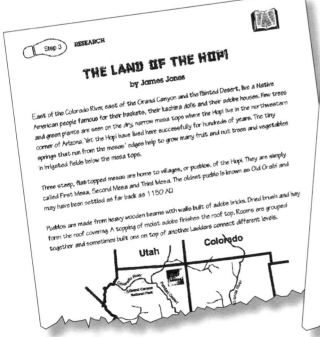

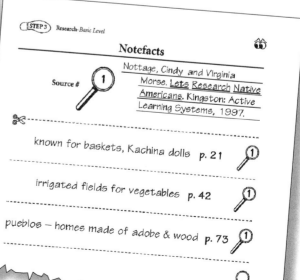

Working Bibliography & Works Cited

Use the MLA documentation style below in developing your:

1. *Working bibliography* – a record of all sources used in your research.

2. *Works cited* – a list of all sources that you cite in the text of your paper.

Print Sources

BOOK: Author(s). <u>Title</u>. City of publication: Publisher, Date.

Parker, Derek and Julia Barker. <u>Atlas of the Supernatural</u>. New York: Prentice Hall, 2000.

CHART, MAP, OR POSTER: <u>Title</u>. Map, chart, or poster. City of publication: Publisher, Date.

<u>The Solar System</u>. Poster. Palo Alto: Dale Seymour Publications, 2007

ENCYCLOPEDIA AND REFERENCE BOOKS: Author(if given) or editor (ed.). "Title of article." <u>Title of book or publication</u>. edition year.

Pope, Clifford. "Crocodile." <u>Encyclopedia Americana.</u> 2004 ed.

MAGAZINE: Author(s). "Title of article." <u>Name of magazine.</u> Date: Page numbers.

Satchell, Michael. "To Save the Sequoias." <u>U.S News and World Report.</u> 7 Oct. 2006: 42-46.

NEWSPAPER: Author. "Title of article." <u>Name of Newspaper</u> [City if not part of name] Date, edition (if listed): Page(s).

Murphy, Sean. "It Floats." <u>Rockingham News</u> [Exeter] 21 May 2009, late ed.: A1+.

PAMPHLET: Same style as book

Non-Print Sources

FIELD TRIP: Site. Location. Attending Group. Date.

Longfellow-Evangeline State Commemorative Area. St. Martinville, LA. Grade 6, Maplewood Middle School. 13 March 2007.

INTERVIEW: Person interviewed. Type of interview (personal, telephone. . .). Date.

Parsons, Mary. Telephone interview. 30 May 2008.

Working Bibliography & Works Cited *(cont.)*

SOUND RECORDINGS: Artist. <u>Title of selection</u>. Medium (unless CD). Manufacturer, Date.

> Kawamura, Masako. <u>Baratata-Batake</u>. Audiocassette. PWS Records, 1996.

SPEAKER: Speaker. "Title." Sponsoring organization. Location. Date.

> Landry, Bob. "Acadiens." Maplewood 6th Grade Team. Maplewood Middle School Auditorium, Sulphur, LA. 7 March 2009.

TELEVISION OR RADIO PROGRAM: "Title of episode or segment." Performer, narrator, director, or author. <u>Title of program</u>. Network. Call letters, City, Date(s).

> "Secrets of Lost Empires." <u>Nova</u>. PBS. WGBH, Boston, 26 May 2007.

VIDEO: <u>Title</u>. Director or producer. Medium (unless film). Distributor, Date.

> <u>Jurassic Park, The Lost World</u>. Dir. Stephen Speilberg. Videocassette. Century Fox, 1995.

Electronic Sources

CD-ROM: Author (if given). "Title of section." <u>Title of publication</u>. CD-ROM. edition, release, or version. City of publication: Publisher, Year.

> "Whiskey Rebellion." <u>Microsoft Encarta</u>. CD-ROM. 2006 ed. New York: Funk & Wagnalls, 2006.

WEB PAGE: Author. "Title." Date of posting or latest update. Site sponsor or Internet site. Date of access <Electronic address or URL>.

> Morse, Sarah. "Female Pedagogy." 25 May 2008. Morse Homepage. 3 August 2009 <http://www.morsefamily.com>.

ENTIRE WEB SITE: <u>Title of web site</u>. Editor (if given). Date of posting or latest update. Name of sponsoring organization. Date of access <Electronic address or URL>.

> <u>Building Green Homes</u>. Harold House. 4 June 2008. Green Living. 30 April 2009 <http://greenliving.org>.

NOTE 1: You may use italics instead of the underlining used in the samples. Check with your teacher to see if there is a preference.

NOTE 2: For more detailed directions and complete listings, see <u>MLA Handbook for Writers of Research Papers</u> (Gibaldi 2009).

NOTE 3: You might want to use an electronic citation site. Be sure you have recorded all the necessary information while you are working on your notes. Two free sites are: Citation machine—<u>http://citationmachine.net</u> and Easy Bib—<u>www.easybib.com</u>

Notefacts

Source #

Basic
Workpages

Notefacts

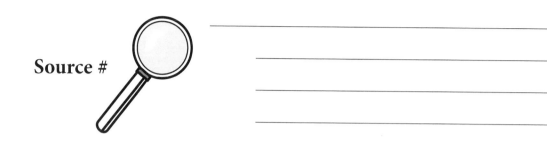

Source #

- -

Labeled Diagram

Basic Workpages

Notefacts

Source #

Notefacts

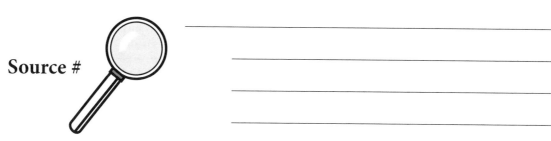

Source #

Labeled Diagram

Sources of Information

Writing Organized Notefacts

Notes About _____

Writing Organized Notefacts

<u>**Notes About**</u>

Labeled Diagram

Notefact Grid

Name:

Topic:

TITLE OF RESOURCE

Source 1:

Source 2:

Source 3:

Write up to 6 key notefacts in each column. Record the source number in the box for each notefact.

Question/Category	Question/Category	Question/Category

Steps to Organizing

1. Think about categories as you read **all** your notefacts.
2. List categories at the bottom of this page.
3. Color the **handle** of each category lens a different color.
4. Write categories on *Organizing Notefacts* pages, one sheet for each category.

Notes About _____   Your category color

(Your category name)

5. Color code all your notefacts according to category colors. (Color handle only.)
6. Cut notefact strips.
7. Place color-coded notefact strips on each *Organizing Notefacts* page.
8. Rearrange the notefacts in an order that makes sense.
9. Check with your teacher.
10. Glue strips to pages.

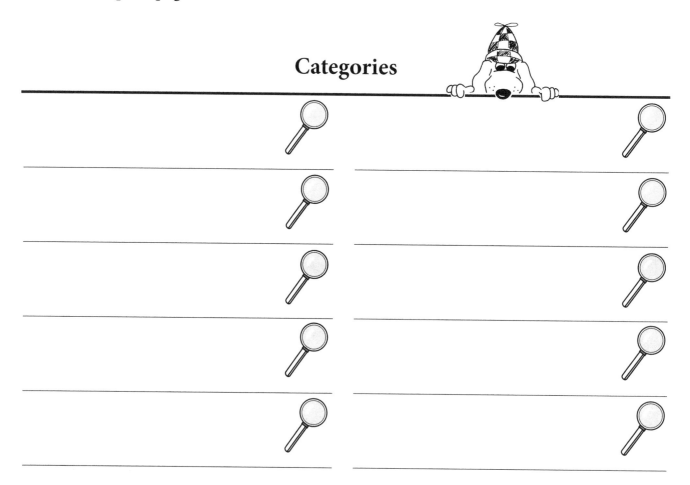

Categories

Basic Workpages

Organizing Notefacts

Notes About_____

Attach your notefacts here

Evaluating Research Goals *What I Learned*

Notefact Goal: _____   Notefacts Written: _____

Required Number of Glossary Entries: _____   Number of Glossary Entries: _____

Required Number of Resources: _____   Number of Resources Used: _____

Required Resource Types: _____ _____ _____ _____

Goal Achieved (check): ☐   ☐   ☐   ☐

Key Findings About My Topic

What are the most important findings you would like to share with others when you reach Step 6 -Product?

1. _____

_____

_____

2. _____

_____

_____

3. _____

_____

_____

My Key Glossary Words: _____

_____

_____

My Future IIM Goals: _____

_____

_____

_____

_____

Possible Goals

Number of note-facts, notefact quality, number of resources, resource types, goal setting questions, time management...

Evaluating Research Goals *Using a Thesis Statement*

Notefact Goal: _____ Notefacts Written: _____

Required Number of Glossary Entries: _____ Number of Glossary Entries: _____

Required Number of Resources: _____ Number of Resources Used: _____

Required Resource Types: _____ _____ _____ _____

Goal Achieved (check): ☐ ☐ ☐ ☐

My Thesis Statement: _____

_____

Were you able to prove your Thesis Statement? _____

Write a paragraph showing the information you gathered that supports this conclusion.

_____

_____

_____

_____

_____

_____

_____

My Future IIM Goals: _____

_____

_____

_____

Possible Goals

Number of note-facts, notefact quality, number of resources, resource types, goal setting questions, time management...

Choosing a Product

Your product must show what you've learned during IIM. Choose something:
- *that you enjoy* • *that will be interesting to others*
- *that is different from other products you've made*

Action: commercial, competition, dance, debate, demonstration, experiment, game, interview, lesson, performance, play, puppet show, scavenger hunt, speech, treasure hunt,

Collection: collage, display, learning center, mini-museum, portfolio, scrapbook, terrarium,

Model: diorama, invention, musical instrument, scale model, sculpture,

Technology: animation, computer program, database, overhead projection, photograph, radio program, slide/sound program, tape recording, TV program, video tape, web page,

Visual Representation: bulletin board, cartoon, chart, concept map, costume, display board, family tree, flag, float, graph, map, mask, mobile, mural, needlework, painting, picture book, poster, project cube, puzzle, quilt, time line,

Written Work: advertisement, book (ABC, biography, diary, fact, fantasy, flip book, journal, picture book, recipe book, science fiction, shape book), brochure, crossword puzzle, dictionary, fact cards, letter, magazine, news report, poetry, riddle, song, travel log, word search,

Remember!
- Be sure your product shares what you've learned during your research
- Plan carefully
- Leave enough time to make a quality product
- Proofread your work

Change any of the suggestions, or come up with your own ideas.

My Product

Product: _____

List the steps you will follow in making your product:

_____   _____

_____   _____

_____   _____

List the materials you will need:

_____   _____

_____   _____

_____   _____

What problem(s) might keep you from completing your product?

_____   _____

_____   _____

Use this space (or the back of the page) to draw a diagram of your product.

Be sure to label
your diagram!

My IIM Product Tally

Name: _____

Product Types

Action...Collection...
Model...Technology
Visual Representation...
Written Work

Keep a dated record of the products you make in your IIMs. Refer to *Choosing a Product* to help you choose a variety of products.

Date	Topic	Product Type	Product

My Presentation

Product: _____

Method of Presentation: *(Describe and list steps)*

_____

_____

_____

_____

_____

_____

Materials I Will Need:

☐ Notecards   ☐ Handout—attach copy

☐ Visual Aids—list: ☐ Equipment—list:

_____   _____

_____   _____

_____   _____

 ## Last Chance Check!
1. Practice your presentation.
2. Evaluate both your product and presentation.
3. Circle what you have done well.
4. Improve those things that aren't circled.

My Product:

Teaches something I've learned

Uses correct spelling and grammar

Is a creative way to share information

My Presentation:

Teaches something I've learned

Is clear and well organized

Uses quality speaking voice: slow, clear, and loud

Is interesting to audience

Fact Gathering *from Presentations*

Name: _____

Be an active listener. For each presentation, write the presenter's name(s), topic, and 3 key facts you want to remember.

Presenter(s)	Fact 1	Fact 2	Fact 3
Name _____ Topic _____			
Name _____ Topic _____			
Name _____ Topic _____			
Name _____ Topic _____			

Write several open-ended questions that you can answer from your research to help your audience learn about your topic.

Ask Me These Questions

SECTION THREE

IIM - Basic Level
Sample Research Study
Using the Independent IIM Process

This sample IIM research study has been developed to help you understand the use of the *IIM Unit Plan* and the Student Workpages at the Basic Level. This dinosaur unit models a third grade class study. The student work reflects the skills of a typical third grade student.

The unit plan includes academic and study skills objectives based on state standards. There are "How to" skills that need to be taught as well as assessment strategies that relate directly to the objectives. The list of teacher resources are representative of what might be available in most schools and contains books and videos you could use. Allison's resources are our creation.

For this model student booklet, the teacher has chosen the sample pages referenced in the Teacher/Student steps in Section One. There are additional pages in Section Two you might choose if you are working with students in higher grades or those experienced in IIM who are ready for more advanced skills. These include developing and defending a thesis statement, asking questions based on Bloom's Taxonomy, and writing notefacts by category. You will also find an alternative cover page and notefact pages with narrower line spacing. (See page references under Teacher Tips for each step.)

CONTENTS - SECTION THREE

Dinosaur Unit Plan 74
Student Booklet. 79

✔ Objectives, Skills, & Standards
IIM Unit Plan

Curriculum Unit: Dinosaurs

Class: Grade 3   Ted Rex

Dates: March 1-26

Time: Lang. Arts/Science/Art/
Library class periods

Process Used (circle):   *Basic Group*   (*Basic Independent*)   *Proficient Group*   *Proficient Independent*

Academic and Study Skills Objectives:

Students will:

Learn the 7 steps of Independent IIM

Learn specific information about dinosaurs, adaptations, habitats, and
inherited characteristics

Take notefacts without plagiarizing

Take notefacts from a video

Learn key vocabulary words related to topic chosen

Present big book to Grade 1 classes

Teacher Essential Question(s):

How does habitat impact survival?

UNIT FOCUS QUESTIONS

What was your dinosaur's habitat?

Why was your dinosaur able to survive in this habitat?

Describe the life cycle of your dinosaur.

"How To" Skills:

Teach students "How to":

Complete each of 7 steps (using Triceratops as my model)

Gather relevant information from video

Lay out book page - title, illustration, text. Use stencil letters

Use appropriate voice tone and rate of speech with microphone when presenting to Grade 1

Use big book page to clarify message

Standards Addressed:

Identify organisms that once lived and that have disappeared (MA, Sci., Strand 2)

Explain how structures are related to the survival of that organism (NH, Life Sci., Std. 3)

Organize and convey information effectively in written reports (VT, Comm., 1.8)

Speak appropriately to different audiences for different purposes and occasions (TX, Eng., 3.3)

Generate questions/conduct research using information from many sources (TX, Eng., 3.12A-J)

Develop an extensive vocabulary (TX, Eng., 3.8 A-D)

Resources
IIM Unit Plan

Curriculum Unit: Dinosaurs

List the resources you will use during the unit. Be sure to include some that are appropriate for the diverse learning needs and styles within your classroom.

Print: (book, computer, poster...)

Norman, David and Angela Milner. *Dinosaur*. New York: Alfred A. Knopf, 1989.

Poster set

My collection of dinosaur books, posters, fact cards

Non-Print: (field trip, video, experiment...)

Fossils: Windows into the Past. Videocassette, Rainbow Educational Media, 1999.

Acton Discovery Museum, Acton, MA

My dinosaur models

People: (speaker, parent volunteer, other teacher...)

Ms. Barbara Brush - art teacher - big book page layout and design

Dr. James Jurassic - science professor - Astute Academy

Ms. Paige - librarian - introduce non-book resources, research time

Ms. Trish Triassic - Title I tutor - Steps 3 - 6

Mr. Ron Raptor - enrichment specialist - book cover and binding with arts cluster group, paleontology extension studies with g/t students

Parent volunteers - field trip, Steps 3 & 4

Preparatory Activities/Materials:

Student Booklet Pages: Sec. 2: p. 39, 40, 41, 44, 46, 51-54, 62-64, 66, 67, 69, 205, 208, 209

Transparencies: All student booklet pages to use for model lessons

Other: Set presentation date/time

Fill in student booklet information

before copying

Immersion Activities: Trip to Acton

Discovery Museum, Interest center

Assessment
IIM Unit Plan

Curriculum Unit: Dinosaurs

What *process skills* will you assess?

Vocabulary development

Quantity and quality of notefacts

The relationship of goal setting questions to research information

Presentation skills

7 Steps of research

How?

Use of 5 key vocabulary words in writing sample

Rubric (Sec. 7: p. 208)

Grade *Evaluating Research Goals* (Sec. 2: p. 64)

1st grade teachers complete rubric (Sec. 7: p. 205) for voice tone, rate of speech, presentation of big book page

Informal assessment using daily journal entries

What *products* will you assess?

Authenticity of illustration and page layout in big book page

How?

Class rubric (Sec. 7: p. 209)

7 Steps
IIM Unit Plan

Curriculum Unit: Dinosaurs

List what you will do for each step of the process. Include unit activities, assessment strategies, and skills lessons. Identify ways you will differentiate for the diverse learning needs and styles of your students.

Step 1 Topic

With class, develop two chart webs: Dinosaur Facts and Dinosaur Fiction

Class visits Acton Discovery Museum dinosaur exhibit

With class, list possible research topics and have students choose their own

Mr.Raptor, enrichment teacher, works 2x /week with advanced reading group on topic choice

in paleontology; differentiates each step of process

Students make individual web for own topic referring to class dinosaur fact and fiction webs

Have students begin to identify and record key words for their study (Sec 2: p. 45)

Step 2 Goal Setting

Show students goals for the study (Sec 2: p. 46)

Students set personal notefact goal and write goal setting questions

Work with class on asking good questions (skills lesson)

Step 3 Research

Give after-school training to parents who will help in class

3 parents help with each research session

Introduce paraphrasing from text (skills lesson)

Teach use of *Notefacts* pages

Ms. Paige, librarian, introduces non-book resources

7 Steps
IIM Unit Plan

STEP 4 Organizing

Play category game "Bird, Beast, or Fish"

Introduce *Steps to Organizing*

2 parents help with each organizing session

STEP 5 Goal Evaluation

Students complete Sec. 2: p. 64

Students choose information that will be presented in text and illustration of big book page

Use rubric, Sec 7: p. 208 to assess work from Step 3 - Research

STEP 6 Product

With class, develop quality standards chart for book page (skills lesson)

Ms. Brush, art teacher, instructs students on how to lay out a book page and in use of
  stencil letters (skills lesson)

Check for accuracy of facts and authenticity of illustration on *My Product* page

Mr. Raptor works with arts cluster students on cover and binding of book

Use rubric, Sec 7: p. 209, to evaluate big book page

STEP 7 Presentation

Students practice reading orally with microphone and displaying book to classmates
  (skills lesson)

Students read pages of big book to Grade 1 classes in auditorium

1st grade teachers and classmates use rubric, Sec 7: p. 205, to evaluate presentation

Independent Investigation Method ®

Hi! I'm Agent

Agent

Name: Allison
Saurus

STUDENT BOOKLET
Basic Level

By: Allison Saurus

Grade: 3

Teacher: Mr. Ted Rex

Class IIM Unit

Dinosaurs

My IIM Topic

Pteranodon

Date Started: March 1

Date Finished: March 26

Basic
Sample Study

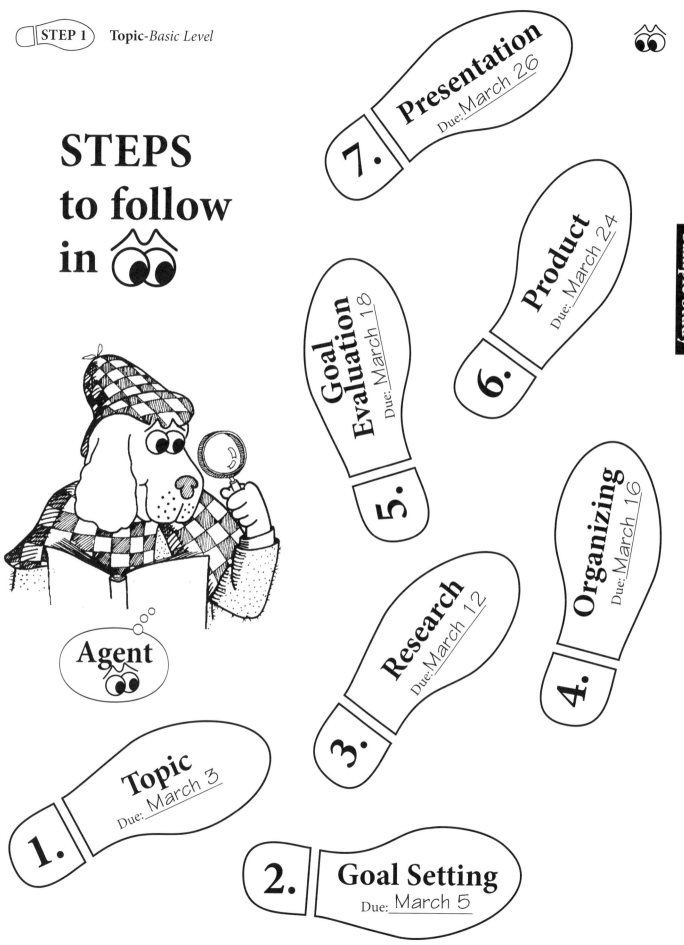

STEPS
to follow
in 👀

Agent

1. Topic
Due: March 3

2. Goal Setting
Due: March 5

3. Research
Due: March 12

4. Organizing
Due: March 16

5. Goal Evaluation
Due: March 18

6. Product
Due: March 24

7. Presentation
Due: March 26

Basic Sample Study

Concept Map

Web ideas about your *Topic* on the *Concept Map* using what you already know and questions about what you want to learn.

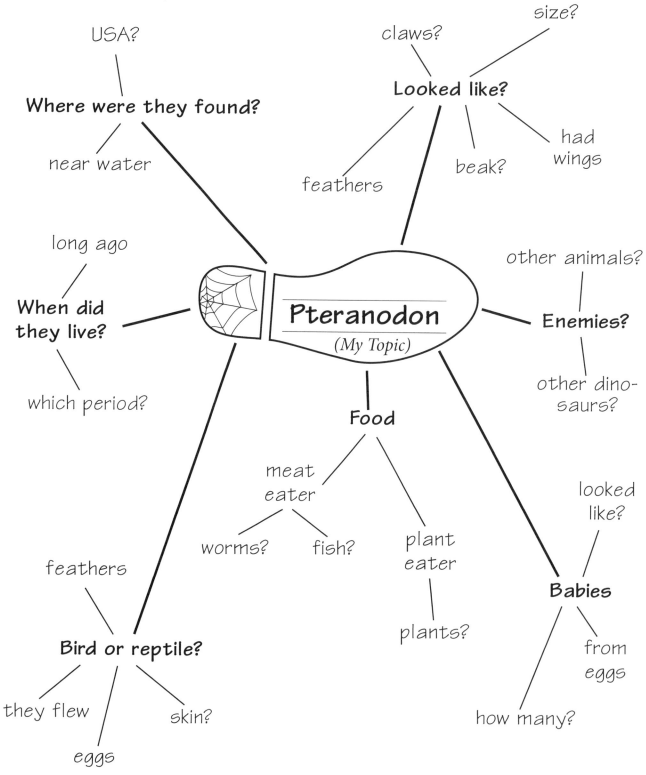

USA?

Where were they found?

near water

claws?   size?

Looked like?

feathers   beak?   had wings

long ago

When did they live?

which period?

Pteranodon
(My Topic)

other animals?

Enemies?

other dino-
saurs?

Food

meat
eater

worms?   fish?

plant
eater

plants?

looked
like?

Babies

from
eggs

how many?

feathers

Bird or reptile?

they flew   skin?

eggs

Setting Research Goals

Notefact Goal: _____ 35 _____

Required Glossary Entries: _____ 5 _____

Required Number of Resources: _____ 3 _____

Required Resource Types: _____ Video _____

_____ Book _____

_____ Computer _____

Resource Types

Book, magazine, Internet, TV show, letter, computer, interview, video/movie, poster, field trip...

Basic Sample Study

My Topic: _____

Questions to Guide My Research
Teacher Question(s):

_____ How does habitat impact survival? _____

_____ What was your dinosaur's habitat? _____

_____ Why was your dinosaur able to survive in this habitat? ____

_____ Describe the life cycle of your dinosaur. _____

_____

_____

_____

My Questions:

_____ What were its enemies? _____

_____ What did it eat? _____

_____ Where have they found fossils? _____

_____ When did it live? _____

_____ Was it a bird? _____

_____

_____

Glossary of the Study

List the NEW words and their meanings that are key to the understanding of your topic.

omnivore	animal that feeds on plants and other animals
Pterosaur	Greek for winged reptile; family of reptiles that lived from late Triassic to end of Cretaceous period
crest	tuft of feathers or bony bump on head of an animal, especially a bird
extinct	no longer existing
adaptation	changes an animal makes to help it survive in its environment
reptile	coldblooded animal with backbone that crawls or moves on short legs, usually hatches from an egg

Notefacts

Source #

<u>When Dinosaurs Ruled the Earth.</u>

<u>Dir. Stephen Stego. DVD.</u>

<u>Century Fox, 2005.</u>

Pteranodon — furry body, size of turkey

soared over water hunting fish

ate fish

males larger than females

excellent glider

spindly hind legs

toothless ①

good eyesight ①

couldn't smell well ①

lived in colonies ①

used crest for rudder ②

bones found in USA (Kansas) ②

not good walker on land ③

Basic Sample Study

Notefacts

Source #

Jurassic, James. <u>Prehistoric Creatures</u>. Exeter: Seaside Publishing, 2006.

Lived in Jurassic & Cretaceous periods

Jurassic period—
200,000,000 to 136,000,000 years ago

Cretaceous period—
136,000,000 to 65,000,000 years ago

Cretaceous ones flew better than Jurassics

flying reptile

skin covered with thin hair

Notefacts

Source #

Cretaceous, Carla._"Flying
Reptiles." The Dinosaur Digest.
31 July 2009: 42-44.

Labeled Diagram

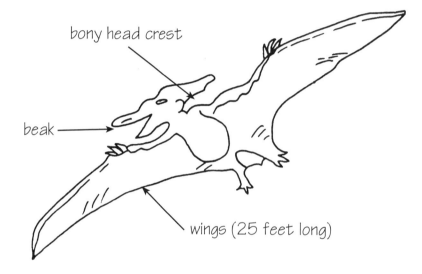

bony head crest

beak

wings (25 feet long)

bony head crest

claws on fingers and toes

lived by seaside cliffs

Assessment
Moving from 1-4 Rubric: *(Step or Skill)*   **Research**

Name(s): _____ Allison Saurus _____

Topic: _____ Pteranodon _____ Date: ___ March 15 ___

For the Teacher: Create with class or assign criteria and indicators for quality work. If you decide to give a grade, use the total possible points to decide on a range for letter grades.

1. Criterion: ____ Quantity of Notefacts _____

Indicators: ____ At least 30 notefacts _____

1 _____ 2 _____ 3 _____ ④

2. Criterion: ____ Quality of Notefacts _____

Indicators: ____ Not copied, enough information, short, related to goal setting questions. __

1 _____ 2 _____ ③ _____ 4

3. Criterion: ____ Number of resources _____

Indicators: ____ At least 3 _____

1 _____ 2 _____ 3 _____ ④

4. Criterion: ____ Types of resources _____

Indicators: ____ At least 3 _____

1 _____ ② _____ 3 _____ 4

Grading

A = __15 – 16__   **D** = __9 – 10__

B = __13 – 14__   **Not**   Less

C = __11 – 12__   **Yet** = __than 9__

Final Grade = _____ B _____

Ratings

1 = Just Beginning   **3** = Made It

2 = Moving Up   **4** = Over the Top

Steps to Organizing

1. Think about categories as you read **all** your notefacts.

2. List categories at the bottom of this page.

3. Color the **handle** of each category lens a different color.

4. Write categories on *Organizing Notefacts* pages, one sheet for each category.

Notes About _____ (Your category name)
→ Your category color

5. Color code all your notefacts according to category colors. (Color handle only.)

6. Cut notefact strips.

7. Place color-coded notefact strips on each *Organizing Notefacts* page.

8. Rearrange the notefacts in an order that makes sense.

9. Check with your teacher.

10. Glue strips to pages.

Categories

food

habitat

enemies

what it looked like

relatives

when it lived

Organizing Notefacts

Notes About ___what it looked like___

Attach your notefacts here

Pteranodon—furry body, size of turkey ①

toothless ①

bony head crest ③

claws on fingers and toes ③

Labeled Diagram

bony head crest

beak

claws

wings (25 feet long)

③

Evaluating Research Goals *What I Learned*

Notefact Goal: 35   Notefacts Written: 37

Required Number of Glossary Entries: 5   Number of Glossary Entries: 6

Required Number of Resources: 3   Number of Resources Used: 4

Required Resource Types: _Video_   _Book_   _Computer_

Goal Achieved (check): ☑   ☑   ☐   ☐

Key Findings About My Topic

What are the most important findings you would like to share with others when you reach Step 6 -Product?

1. It used its 25 ft. wings for gliding up to cliffs and for soaring over the water hunting fish.

2. Most of its food – fish, snails, shrimp-like shell fish, sand fleas, and red algae – came from the water and the shores.

3. It adapted to its environment by using its head crest like a rudder to move towards the fish it caught with its big beak and sharp claws.

My Key Glossary Words: omnivore, crest, adaptation, reptile

My Future IIM Goals: I will use the computer and more resources. I will finish my research earlier so I can spend more time on my product.

Possible Goals

Number of note-facts, notefact quality, number of resources, resource types, goal setting questions, time management...

Choosing a Product

Your product must show what you've learned during IIM. Choose something:

- *that you enjoy* • *that will be interesting to others*
- *that is different from other products you've made*

Action: commercial, competition, dance, debate, demonstration, experiment, game, interview, lesson, performance, play, puppet show, scavenger hunt, speech, treasure hunt,

Collection: collage, display, learning center, mini-museum, portfolio, scrapbook, terrarium,

Model: diorama, invention, musical instrument, scale model, sculpture,

Technology: animation, computer program, database, overhead projection, photograph, radio program, slide/sound program, tape recording, TV program, video tape, web page,

Visual Representation: bulletin board, cartoon, chart, concept map, costume, display board, family tree, flag, float, graph, map, mask, mobile, mural, needlework, painting, picture book, poster, project cube, puzzle, quilt, time line,

Written Work: advertisement, book (ABC, biography, diary, fact, fantasy, flip book, journal, picture book, recipe book, science fiction, shape book), brochure, crossword puzzle, dictionary, fact cards, letter, magazine, news report, poetry, riddle, song, travel log, word search,
          page for class big book

> **Remember!**
> - Be sure your product shares what you've learned during your research
> - Plan carefully
> - Leave enough time to make a quality product
> - Proofread your work

**Change any of the suggestions, or
come up with your own ideas.**

My Product

Product: Big book page — Pteranodon

List the steps you will follow in making your product:

1. Write sentences with facts	4. Draw pictures
2. Measure & lay out page	5. Write sentences
3. Stencil in title	6. Proofread, then color

List the materials you will need:

cardboard	stencil letters
ruler	picture of Pteranodon
markers	

What problem(s) might keep you from completing your product?

 Rehearsals for my dance recital might take too much time.

Use this space (or the back of the page) to draw a diagram of your product.

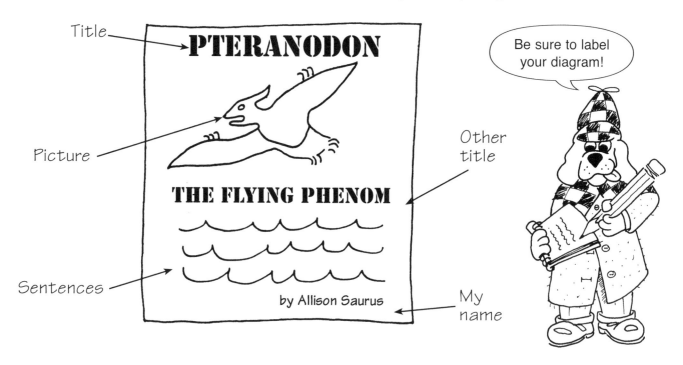

Title — PTERANODON

Picture

THE FLYING PHENOM

Other title

Be sure to label your diagram!

Sentences

by Allison Saurus

My name

Assessment

4 Square Rubric: *(Step or Skill)*

Big Book Page

Name: Allison Saurus   Topic: Pteranodon

For the Teacher: List criteria and indicators for each rating number.

Criterion: Illustration - realistic

1	2	3 ✓	4
Little/no relationship to topic	Some use of color Accurate details	Effective use of color and details	Use of background details to enhance knowledge

Criterion: Writing mechanics - grammar, spelling, punctuation

1	2 ✓	3	4
5+ errors	3 - 4 errors	1 - 2 errors	No errors

Criterion: Research findings - facts on page

1	2	3 ✓	4
0 - 2	3 - 5	6 - 8	9 +

Criterion: Page layout - design elements

1	2	3 ✓	4
Random design	Some design plan	Effective use of measurement, spacing, text, and illustrations	Creative design enhances understanding

My IIM Product Tally

Name: _Allison Saurus_

Keep a dated record of the products you make in your IIMs. Refer to *Choosing a Product* to help you choose a variety of products.

Product Types

Action...Technology...
Collection...Visual
Representation...Model...
Written Work...

Date	Topic	Product Type	Product
10/2/08	Pilgrims	Visual	Mural
12/16/09	Weather	Technology	Power Point
3/26/09	Pteranodon	Written	Big book page

My Presentation

Product: Big book page

Method of Presentation: *(Describe and list steps)*

I will put my big book page on the
easel. I will face the class and tell
them what I studied (notecard). Then
I'll point to page with pointer while I read
the words.

Materials I Will Need:

☑ Notecards

☑ Visual Aids—list:

big book page

☐ Handout—attach copy

☑ Equipment—list:

pointer, microphone
easel

Last Chance Check!
1. Practice your presentation.
2. Evaluate both your product and presentation.
3. Circle what you have done well.
4. Improve those things that aren't circled.

My Product:
(Teaches something I've learned)
Uses correct spelling and grammar
(Is a creative way to share information)

My Presentation:
(Teaches something I've learned)
(Is clear and well organized)
Uses quality speaking voice: slow,
clear, and loud
(Is interesting to audience)

Assessment
Criteria List Rubric: *(Step or Skill)*   **Presentation**

Name(s): Allison Saurus

Topic: Pteranodon   Date: March 26

Name of Peer Evaluator: Sarah Tops

For the Teacher: Create with class or assign criteria for quality work. If you decide to give a grade, use the total possible points to decide on a range for letter grades.

CRITERIA	STUDENT OR PEER	TEACHER	COMMENT
Shows knowledge of topic	4	3	I counted 10 facts
Organized	3	2	Practice holding cards
			and microphone
Interesting	4	3	
Quality visuals	3	3	
Uses imagination & creativity	4	4	Great costume!
Good voice tone	4	3	Be sure to look at the
			audience
Makes eye contact	2	2	
TOTAL	24	20	= 44

Grading

A = 50 - 56   **D** = 30 - 36

B = 44 - 49   **Not**

C = 37 - 43   **Yet** = Below 30

Final Grade = ___B___

Ratings

1 = Just Beginning   **3** = Made It

2 = Moving Up   **4** = Over the Top

SECTION FOUR

IIM - Proficient Level "How To"

The Proficient Level of the Independent Investigation Method has been developed for older students with more research experience. Students may work as a whole class using the Group IIM Process or on individual studies using the Independent IIM Process.

They will build upon the foundation skills learned at the Basic Level, and will use more sophisticated research techniques found on the Student Workpages in Section Five. This is a rigorous process and not appropriate for all students.

The plans for you to follow for both the Group IIM Process and the Independent IIM Process are found on the pages for the 7 steps. Each one includes:

 Teacher Steps = what you should do at each of the seven steps,

 Student Steps = student behaviors,

 Teacher Tips = words of wisdom from the many teachers who have worked with IIM, and

(•) **CD Tips** = notes for teachers using the IIM Companion CD

CONTENTS - SECTION FOUR

Group IIM Process Overview... 101
Group IIM Process 7 Steps. 103
Independent IIM Process Overview.. 111
Independent IIM Process 7 Steps 113

Proficient Level

Group IIM Process
(A Whole-Class Study)

OVERVIEW

By using the Proficient Level of the Group IIM Process for a whole-class study, you can introduce older students to IIM in 7 days and have them ready to research independently. This is also an effective review technique with younger students who have had some experience with IIM. Choose a topic from your regular curriculum unit to use as the model for this group process.

Teacher Example:

CLASS UNIT: Native Americans

GROUP TOPIC: Hopi

INDEPENDENT TOPICS: Other Native American tribes

Prepare the teacher and team sets referenced in the Teacher Steps and Student Steps. Your class will work in teams of 3-4 to research the same topic following the 7 steps of IIM. While working in groups, students will practice using the Student Workpages from the Basic Level of the Independent IIM Process. In Step 3, it is important to choose a different resource type for each team to use in their research. During Step 4, each team will organize a set of duplicated notefacts. For Product and Presentation (Steps 6 & 7), the class will focus on 5 of the Multiple Intelligences as they design and present team products from the same notefacts. At the end of this study, students are ready to research independently at the Basic or Proficient Level.

The teacher and team sets needed for the Proficient Level Group IIM Process can be customized and printed out using the IIM Companion CD.

SYNOPSIS
Proficient Level – Group IIM Process

STEP 1 Topic *Day 1*
The teacher works with students to develop a concept map on a topic from the class unit.

STEP 2 Goal Setting *Day 1*
The teacher leads students in developing good questions to frame the class research study.

STEP 3 Research *Day 2 & 3*
After the teacher models taking notefacts from two types of resources, students work in teams to take their own notefacts from other resources.

STEP 4 Organizing *Day 4*
Student teams organize all notefacts from sources #1, #2 and #3.

STEP 5 Goal Evaluation *Day 4*
The class evaluates knowledge acquisition and research process skills.

STEP 6 Product *Day 5 & 6*
Each student team makes a product to share what they have learned.

STEP 7 Presentation *Day 6*
The teams present products to the class.

NEXT STEP Independent IIM *Day 7*
Students are ready to begin independent or small group IIMs using topics from the same or a future class unit.

Proficient Level Group IIM Process
STEP 1-Topic – *Day 1*

Teacher Steps

The teacher will:

a. Choose unit of study from regular curriculum
b. Choose topic from this unit
c. Fill out *IIM Unit Plan* for group study (Sec. 5: p. 125-129)
d. Choose 6 resources of different types
e. Immerse students in unit topic using books, interest centers, bulletin boards, posters, experiments, models, filmstrips, videos, speakers, field trips...
f. Introduce students to process by showing IIM vocabulary and steps
g. Have students put information on individual concept maps (Sec. 2: p. 44)
h. With student input, build class concept map about topic

Student Steps

The students will:

a. Participate in immersion activities you choose which introduce topic
b. Develop individual concept maps about topic
c. Contribute to class concept map
d. Add information from overhead to individual concept map

Teacher Tips

- Choose an introductory exploratory activity that will catch the attention of your students.
- Choose a topic for your group study that has a variety of resource types available that relate to your key questions developed from academic objectives.
- Build your class concept map on chart paper, an overhead, a SmartBoard, or by using other tech tools.
- ⊙ Selected student workpages can be customized and printed in collated team booklets using the IIM Companion CD.

Proficient Level Group IIM Process
STEP 2-Goal Setting – *Day 1*

Teacher Steps

The teacher will:

a. Use Teacher Essential Questions from *IIM Unit Plan* (Sec. 5: p. 125) to guide goal setting session

b. Help students formulate good questions by listing teacher and class questions

c. Star 3-5 key goal setting questions to guide research

d. Assign common reading selection, copied for highlighting, to answer goal setting questions either as homework assignment or in-class activity

e. Make copies of finalized goal setting questions for each student

Student Steps

The students will:

a. Work with you to formulate good questions

b. Identify 3-5 key goal setting questions

c. Read and highlight assigned selection, focusing on goal setting questions

Teacher Tips

- Be sure the goal setting questions reflect the sophistication and ability level of your students.

- Keep the focus of the study narrow enough so the questions are researchable and the information is specific.

Proficient Level Group IIM Process
STEP 3-Research – *Days 2 & 3*

Teacher Steps

The teacher will:

a. Introduce/review *Steps to Taking Notefacts* (Sec. 2: p. 49)
b. Demonstrate bibliography format (Sec. 2: p. 50-51)
c. Model notefacts using assigned reading selection as Source #1
d. Model another resource type as Source #2
e. Form student teams of 3-4 students
f. Give each team a different resource type (video, poster, Internet, newspaper, book, magazine…) as Source #3 and a notefact sheet (Sec. 2: p. 55-57)
g. Plan in-class time for students to gather no more than 10 notefacts from team resource
h. Copy a set of all notefacts for each team from teacher Sources #1 and #2
i. Put together one organizing set for each team to use in Step 4: *Steps to Organizing* (Sec. 2: p. 62), teacher-modeled notefacts (sources 1& 2), and at least 4 blank *Organizing Notefacts* pages (Sec. 2: p. 63)

Student Steps

The students will:

a. Contribute notefacts from assigned reading selection during model notefact lesson
b. As a team, take no more than 10 notefacts from assigned resource on team notefact sheets
c. Proofread pages for completeness: assigned source number in all magnifying glasses, accurate facts, bibliography headings

Teacher Tips

- One goal is to show students the many types of resources they should be using when researching.
- Don't be tempted to allow teams to take more than 10 notefacts because there will be too many facts to organize.
- Review cooperative group skills so all students contribute to the team assignments.
- Circulate during team research time to be sure students use proper bibliography and notefact format.
- Your video clip should be short enough to allow time for recording notefacts.
- Class notefacts for sources 1 & 2 can be recorded on and printed from a computer

Proficient Level Group IIM Process
STEP 4-Organizing – *Day 4*

Teacher Steps

The teacher will:

a. Introduce/review *Steps to Organizing* (Sec 2: p.62)

b. Give each team a set of notefacts and *Organizing Notefacts* pages (See h & i, p. 105)

c. Have teams carry out organizing process including their own Source #3 notefacts

d. List on overhead many categories student teams have used for organizing

e. Emphasize variety of team categories and validity of how teams have used the same notefacts in different categories

Student Steps

The students will:

a. As a team, follow *Steps to Organizing* using concept map and goal setting questions to develop categories

b. Share category choices on class chart

c. Justify category choices for notefacts

Teacher Tips

- There is no "right" number of categories. Students do not have to use all the *Organizing Notefacts* sheets they are given.

- Have extra *Organizing Notefacts* sheets available for teams that have many categories.

- Have student teams share reasons for placement of one common notefact to show different category choices for the same notefact.

Proficient Level Group IIM Process
STEP 5-Goal Evaluation – *Day 4*

Teacher Steps

The teacher will:

a. With students, check to see if goal setting questions were answered
b. Use additional formal or informal evaluation techniques if there is time

Student Steps

The students will:

a. Check to see if goal setting questions have been answered
b. Complete additional evaluation activities if assigned

Teacher Tips

- At this point you may want to check knowledge acquisition by giving a quiz or vocabulary test.
- Group debriefing is a good way to have students reflect on the process and group work.
- Students may benefit from forecasting about their readiness to carry out an Independent IIM.
- One of the assessment forms from Section 7 may be used to evaluate teamwork and knowledge acquisition.

Proficient Level Group IIM Process
STEP 6-Product – *Days 5 & 6*

Teacher Steps

The teacher will:

a. Describe/illustrate 5 Intelligences students will use to make team product (Sec. 5: p. 131)

b. Give teams *Product/Presentation Rubric* (Sec. 5: p. 132) with assigned Intelligence listed

c. Provide class time and materials for product development

Student Steps

The students will:

a. Make team product and plan presentation using *Product/Presentation Rubric*

b. Develop product based on research information

Teacher Tips

- Help students understand that the assigned Intelligence may be their strength area or an area where they need to grow.

- If you are not comfortable using Multiple Intelligences classifications, assign a different product to each group. Your goal is to model a variety of product and presentation types.

- The greater the variety of materials available, the more diverse and creative the products will be.

Proficient Level Group IIM Process
STEP 7-Presentation – *Day 6*

Teacher Steps

The teacher will:

a. Have students record information from presentations on *Fact Gathering from Presentations* (Sec. 2: p. 70)

b. Provide time for debriefing including team self-assessment rating

Student Steps

The students will:

a. Present team product

b. Write facts on *Fact Gathering from Presentations* during other team presentations

c. Evaluate own team's product and presentation on rubric

Teacher Tips

- Students are always the teachers in this step.
- If the grid is not used for audience accountability, find/develop some other technique to keep students engaged as active listeners and learners.
- You may want to review what makes a quality audience.
- You can assess student work on the rubric along with the students or instead of the students.
- ⊙ You can add the categories on the *Fact Gathering Grid* and criteria on the Assessment Forms using the IIM Companion CD.

Proficient Level Group IIM Process
NEXT STEP – *Day 7*

Teacher Steps

The teacher will:

Using this or future curriculum unit, assign or let students choose topics for independent or small group IIMs following steps in Basic or Proficient Level of Independent IIM Process

Student Steps

The students will:

Begin individual or small group IIMs on topic of class unit using Basic or Proficient Level of Independent IIM Process

Proficient Level

Independent IIM Process

Overview

You would choose the Proficient Level of the Independent IIM Process after your students have learned the foundation skills of independent research. They will build on the skills used at the Basic Level by conducting a presearch of the literature, formulating a research question, using primary sources, interpreting data, developing conclusions, and sharing their voice through a creative product and/or the proof of their thesis statement in a research paper. Not all secondary students will be able to complete this rigorous process. However, there might even be some high ability elementary students who will need the challenge of the Proficient Level. Since the Basic Level has many advanced pages for experienced researchers, it will be up to you to choose the appropriate level according to students' research experience and academic ability.

In developing your research unit at the Proficient Level, use the *IIM Unit Plan* (Sec. 5: p. 125-130) to identify academic, study skills, and assessment objectives and activities for each step. Students need a 3-ring pocket binder organized with tabs for the 7 steps. This allows them to add pages and store notecards, and enables you to access information easily when notebooks are handed in. In the Teacher/Student Steps, we have referenced the reproducible pages which students will complete during their studies. Section Six shows a sample study at the Proficient Level to help you understand how the Student Workpages are used.

Unit Plans, Student Workpages, and Assessment Forms can be designed and customized on the IIM Companion CD. The CD can also be used effectively for model lessons with a SmartBoard or other projection device.

SYNOPSIS
Proficient Level – Independent IIM Process

STEP 1 Topic
Immersion activities and a presearch of the literature give students enough background information to choose a topic from the class unit and develop a concept map.

STEP 2 Goal Setting
The teacher works with students to set research goals and formulate a Research Question.

STEP 3 Research
Students gather data from primary and secondary sources using source and notefact cards.

STEP 4 Organizing
Students organize, analyze, and interpret their data to draw conclusions about their Research and Focus Questions.

STEP 5 Goal Evaluation
Students reflect on the research process using objective and subjective evaluations.

STEP 6 Product
After students decide on an audience, they choose and develop products that share key findings. The teacher may also require a research paper.

STEP 7 Presentation
Students plan, organize, and present their findings to an audience.

Proficient Level Independent IIM Process
STEP 1-Topic

Teacher Steps

The teacher will:

a. Choose unit of study from regular curriculum

b. Fill out *IIM Unit Plan* (Sec. 5: p. 125-130)

c. Decide due dates for 7 Steps, at which steps students will hand in notebooks, and which items will be graded and recorded on *IIM Research Study Plan* (Sec. 5: p. 136)

d. Plan immersion activities to heighten student interest and awareness of topic

e. Introduce students to process by showing IIM vocabulary and steps

f. Work with students to develop class concept map to identify broad unit questions and associated research topics

g. Have each student read one selection about individual interest area and record information on *Presearch* (Sec. 5: p. 137)

h. Guide students in development of individual concept map on *Developing the Research Topic* (Sec. 5: p. 138)

i Encourage students to record key vocabulary of the discipline on *Glossary of the Study* (Sec. 5: p 139)

Proficient "How To"

Student Steps

The students will:

a. Set up three ring binder with tabs for 7 steps

b. Work with teacher to develop class concept map focusing on possible research topics

c. Choose interest area from class topic

d. Read one selection about interest area and record ideas about possible topics

e. Choose topic and develop individual concept map using prior knowledge and questions

f. Begin to record vocabulary of the discipline

g. Record preliminary information on *Research Study Plan*

Teacher Tips

- Class immersion activities give students some background information about the topic to help them identify possible interest areas to research.

- Presearch reading is necessary to give students background knowledge for narrowing a topic, developing a concept map, Research Question, and Focus Questions.

- To promote deeper thinking on the concept map, encourage students to return to the map at a later time with additional ideas/questions written in a different color.

- Use your CD to design your new unit or modify one you have previously used.

- Print out collated student booklets after customizing selected pages.

Proficient Level Independent IIM Process
STEP 2-Goal Setting

Teacher Steps

The teacher will:

a. Help students complete each section of *Setting Research Goals* (Sec. 5: p. 140-141)

b. Assign required resource number and types using **PROVE** and minimum number of primary sources, notefacts, and glossary entries

c. Guide students as they develop Research Question and supporting Focus Questions

d. Show examples of primary sources

Student Steps

The students will:

a. Choose and/or refine Research Question from *Presearch* and/or *Concept Map* identified in Step 1

b. Write Focus Questions to guide research

c. List resource types, and set goals for notefacts, number of resources, primary sources, and glossary entries

Teacher Tips

- Model how to develop a Research Question from the unit topic using the class concept map.

- Students need to learn how to write Focus Questions that will lead them to information relating to their Research Question.

- The glossary of the study is not a complete vocabulary list of the student's topic. It is a listing of key words critical to understanding the topic.

- The notefact goal is a good way to differentiate the process for your students.

- If students are keeping note cards in an envelope, have them write their research question on it as a reminder of the focus of their study.

- ⊙ Goal Setting pages can be customized to reflect your unit goals.

Proficient Level Independent IIM Process
STEP 3-Research

Teacher Steps

The teacher will:

a. Help students identify key skills needed for gathering data: plan and conduct experiment, set up interview date and write questions, write letters of inquiry, plan field trip...

b. Teach students skills needed for data gathering and recording

c. Teach/model source card, notefact card and notetaking formats using *Taking Notefacts on Note Cards* (Sec. 5: p. 143)

Student Steps

The students will:

a. Set up notefact and source cards using *Taking Notefacts on Note Cards*

b. Identify, plan, and complete research activities using non-print resources: experiment, interview, letter of inquiry, field trip...

c. Document data on note cards

d. Conduct additional research by writing notefacts from print resources

e. Continue to list new key words and meanings on *Glossary of the Study* (Sec. 5: p. 139)

Teacher Tips

- At this level, students should use some primary sources to validate their study.

- Have students practice note-taking skills in different assignments so they become skilled using print, non-print, and action sources.

- Information from action research (interview, survey, experiment, field trip...) must be documented as notefacts.

- If your students have difficulty with note cards, have them take their notefacts using notefact sheets from the Basic Level (Sec. 2: p. 55-57).

- You may assess process skills using an appropriate form from Section 7.

- ⊙ Customize an Assessment Form on your CD to evaluate the quality of your students' notefacts, interview, or other Step 3 process skills.

Proficient Level Independent IIM Process
STEP 4-Organizing

Teacher Steps

The teacher will:

a. Give necessary instruction for each section of *Organizing, Analyzing, and Interpreting Data* (Sec. 5: p. 147-148)

b. Work with students to develop a Thesis Statement related to their Research Question that they can prove with their data

c. Model choice between essential and supplementary notefacts

d. Assign or help students choose appropriate organizer using *Sample Organizers* (Sec. 5: p. 149)

Student Steps

The students will:

a. Sort notefact cards by Focus Questions or subcategories of questions

b. Develop a Thesis Statement which will be proved in their product

c. Decide which notefacts are essential for proving their Thesis Statement

d. Complete appropriate organizer using essential notefacts

e. Write interpretations/conclusions for each Focus Question using organized data

Teacher Tips

- Don't require a set amount of essential notefacts. This will encourage students to classify everything as "essential".

- You may want to give some type of credit for supplementary notefacts. Students could make an appendix, flip chart, collage . . . or receive extra credit for their research grade.

- At this point, students must decide if further research is needed to find more essential notefacts.

- Students' conclusions need to relate to their Research Question and be more than a restatement of the facts.

- A rubric listing essential qualities for a thesis statement will be a powerful tool for this difficult step.

- Customize rubrics from Section 7 on your CD.

Proficient Level Independent IIM Process
STEP 5-Goal Evaluation

Teacher Steps

The teacher will:

a. Have students fill out all sections of *Evaluating Research Goals* (Sec. 5: p. 150-151)

b. Model how to use documentation data to describe major research findings

c. Provide time for students to debrief progress as researchers: small group interactions, whole class discussion...

d. Guide students in self evaluation of their research by identifying key elements in each level of rubric

Student Steps

The students will:

a. Complete *Evaluating Research Goals* , comparing goals set in Step 2 with work accomplished

b. Use research data to document major research findings

c. Self-evaluate research process

d. Work with class or small group to process what has been learned

Teacher Tips

- It is important for students to get feedback from one another before they choose their audience, product, and presentation.

- In their reflections, students should give specific evaluative information that can be used for their next research assignment.

- The *Subjective Evaluation* (Sec. 5: p. 151) is a good summary page for students to use during group debriefing.

- The graphic organizers made in Step 4 Organizing are effective visuals to use when debriefing with peers.

Proficient Level Independent IIM Process
STEP 6-Product

Teacher Steps

The teacher will:

a. Assist students in completing *Developing a Product* (Sec. 5: p. 153-154)
b. Assign or have students choose appropriate audience for sharing important research study information
c. Guide students in choosing product that will effectively impact audience
d. Develop with class or assign criteria for quality product(s)
d. Teach necessary product skills

Student Steps

The students will:

a. Write research paper if assigned (Sec. 5: p. 152)
b. Choose appropriate audience for sharing information
c. Match product type with audience and presentation style
d. Develop and/or follow criteria for quality product
e. Fill out *Developing a Product* and follow plan in making product

Teacher Tips

- Research papers are handed in to the teacher. Research study results should be presented to an audience in a different format.
- Writing a research paper is a very complex process. You need to allot adequate instructional time as well as time for students to produce a quality paper.
- Audience choice and product development must go hand-in-hand. In order to design a product that impacts an audience, students must first decide who their audience is.
- If the product requires specific skills, you may need to give mini-lessons, find a mentor, or locate how-to information in books or electronically to support the student(s).
- Be sure students have product rubrics in advance of developing their products.
- ⊙ Use the IIM Companion CD to design a rubric from the Assessment Forms to assure quality products.

Proficient Level Independent IIM Process
STEP 7-Presentation

Teacher Steps

The teacher will:

a. Help students complete *Presentation of Research Findings* (Sec. 5: p. 155)
b. Develop with class or assign criteria for quality presentation
c. Facilitate planning of time and place for presentation
d. Teach appropriate presentation skills
e. Plan time for students to practice performance presentations

Student Steps

The students will:

a. Develop and/or follow quality criteria for presentation
b. Complete *Presentation of Research Findings*
c. Prepare for presentation using quality criteria guide
d. Present findings to audience
e. Add research study information to *Research Product/Presentation Inventory* (Sec. 5: p. 156)

Teacher Tips

- It is important to work on scheduling for the presentation ahead of time. Students should help in this process.
- Not all presentations are performances, but all need an audience: letter to the editor, submission to a professional journal.
- ⊙ Save the rubrics you design on your IIM Companion CD for future use.

SECTION FIVE

IIM - Proficient Level Reproducible Teacher and Student Workpages

These reproducible pages will provide you with the tools to develop and carry out your IIM units at the Proficient Level. Use the *IIM Unit Plan* to identify goals and objectives, choose resources, design assessment tools, and develop skills lessons. Product and presentation pages for a Group IIM are included. The Student Workpages give your students the structure to complete an independent research study using the Independent IIM Process at the Proficient Level and are appropriate for older students experienced in IIM. The overview of each part of Section Five gives additional information about the use of these pages.

The IIM Companion CD allows all Teacher and Student Workpages to be edited.

CONTENTS - SECTION FIVE

Teacher Workpages Overview 123
IIM Unit Plan 125
Group Proficient MI Product/Presentation 131
Student Workpages Overview 133
Independent IIM Process Student Workpages 135

Proficient Level

IIM Teacher Workpages

OVERVIEW

These reproducible Teacher Workpages have been developed to aid you in unit and skills lesson planning, and in implementing the Group IIM Process at the Proficient Level.

The *IIM Unit Plan* pages are an efficient way of developing, recording, and carrying out the learning objectives you have for your students for either the Group or Independent IIM Process. Use your state/local standards to identify academic and study skills objectives for the unit (p. 125). From these, list "How to" skills that need direct teaching lessons and record those lesson plans on p. 130. Tie your assessment plans (p. 127) to your objectives, and keep a record of key resources needed and used on p. 126. The *7 Steps* pages (p. 128-129) serve as a flow chart of the total unit.

Also included in the Teacher Workpages are descriptions of 5 of the Multiple Intelligences and a rubric (p. 131-132) to be copied for student use during the Product and Presentation steps of the Group IIM Process.

The *IIM Unit Plan*, Assessment Forms, and selected Student Workpages can be customized, saved, and printed out using the IIM Companion CD.

Proficient
Workpages

Objectives, Skills, & Standards
IIM Unit Plan

Curriculum Unit: _____   Class: _____

Dates: _____   Time: _____

Process Used (circle):   *Basic Group*   *Basic Independent*   *Proficient Group*   *Proficient Independent*

Academic and Study Skills Objectives:
Students will:

_____

_____

_____

_____

_____

_____

Teacher Essential Question(s):

_____

_____

_____

_____

"How To" Skills:
Teach students "How to":

_____

_____

_____

_____

Standards Addressed:

_____

_____

_____

_____

_____

Proficient Workpages

Resources
IIM Unit Plan

Curriculum Unit: _____

List the resources you will use during the unit. Be sure to include some that are appropriate for the diverse learning needs and styles within your classroom.

Print: (book, computer, poster...)

_____
_____
_____
_____
_____
_____

Non-Print: (field trip, video, experiment...)

_____
_____
_____
_____

People: (speaker, parent volunteer, other teacher...)

_____
_____
_____
_____

Preparatory Activities/Materials:

Student Booklet Pages: _____

Transparencies: _____

Other: _____

Immersion Activities: _____

Proficient Workpages

Assessment
IIM Unit Plan

Curriculum Unit: _____

What *process skills* will you assess?

How?

What *products* will you assess?

How?

7 Steps
IIM Unit Plan

Curriculum Unit: _____

List what you will do for each step of the process. Include unit activities, assessment strategies, and skills lessons. Identify ways you will differentiate for the diverse learning needs and styles of your students.

Step 1 Topic

Step 2 Goal Setting

Step 3 Research

7 Steps
IIM Unit Plan (cont.)

STEP 4 Organizing

STEP 5 Goal Evaluation

STEP 6 Product

STEP 7 Presentation

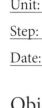

Teaching "How To" Skills
IIM Unit Plan

Use this page to plan mini-lessons to teach key skills during the IIM unit.

Unit: _____

Step: _____ Skill: _____

Date: _____ Class/Time: _____

Objectives:

_____ _____
_____ _____
_____ _____
_____ _____
_____ _____
_____ _____

Materials:

_____ _____
_____ _____
_____ _____
_____ _____
_____ _____
_____ _____

Procedure:

_____ _____
_____ _____
_____ _____
_____ _____
_____ _____
_____ _____

Notes:

_____ _____
_____ _____

MI Descriptors

These descriptions of Multiple Intelligences are based on the work of Dr. Howard Gardner and Dr. Thomas Armstrong. We have chosen 5 of the Intelligences which can be generalized to develop products with any unit.

Verbal - Linguistic (Word Smart)

Description: Uses words effectively both in speaking and writing

Product Types: Word game, puzzle, riddle, rhyme, poem, recitation, debate, speech, dictionary/glossary, reading, writing, or telling a story...

Bodily - Kinesthetic (Body Smart)

Description: Uses body to communicate, solve problems, and make connections through action and movement

Product Types: Crafts, dance, drama, mime, role playing, creative movement, sports...

Logical - Mathematical (Number Smart)

Description: Uses numbers, sequences, patterns, and symbols to communicate and solve problems

Product Types: Word and number problems, strategy game, Venn diagram, graph, chart, time line, experiment...

Visual - Spatial (Picture Smart)

Description: Uses images, color, shape, and form to interpret and share information

Product Types: Model, picture, jigsaw puzzle, map, concept map, building, maze, costume, scenery, poster, diorama...

Proficient Workpages

Musical - Rhythmic (Music Smart)

Description: Uses rhythm, tonal patterns, and pitch to create understanding

Product Types: Information set to tune and rhythm: chant, rap, song, instrumental composition...

Product/Presentation Rubric

Names:_____ _____ _____

_____ _____ _____

Unit: _____ Topic: _____

Using the materials available in the room, your team is to make a

_____

(assigned Intelligence)

product that meets the criteria of the Rating Rubric for your IIM Product/Presentation.

You will have_____ minutes to create and_____minutes to present your product.

Rating for IIM Product/Presentation

CRITERIA	RATING	COMMENT
The Product/ Presentation:		
Shares information about topic		
Uses imagination & creativity		
Is neat		
Displays correct writing mechanics		
Demonstrates assigned Intelligence		
Is well-organized		
Uses good voice tone/eye contact		

Proficient Workpages

Ratings

1 = Just Beginning   **3** = Made It

2 = Moving Up   **4** = Over the Top

NA = Not applicable

Proficient Level

IIM Student Workpages

OVERVIEW

These reproducible Student Workpages have been developed for the Independent Process to guide your students through the 7 steps of IIM at the Proficient Level. They serve as the structure of the study. Since these students are able to work independently, all student pages contain both directions and samples. You will need to decide where to use direct teaching lessons based on your students' research experience and academic level. Refer back to Section Four for a more detailed explanation of the Student Workpages to help with those decisions.

To maintain the integrity of the research method, students should complete a product to share with an audience. A research paper should not be used as a presentation product but may be completed and turned in for grading. *Writing a Research Paper* (p. 152) is included to help students with this process.

The IIM Companion CD may be used to customize the Student Workpages for student booklets or for use in model lessons. It also is an effective teaching tool using a SmartBoard or another electronic projection device.

IIM®
Independent Investigation Method

IIM RESEARCH STUDY
Proficient Level

Name:

IIM Research Study Plan

This is your plan to keep records of each step of your IIM. Start with *Name, Class,* and *Class Topic*. Add date goals set in class or by your teacher. Then fill in each section as you complete the step. This allows you to stay on task and chart your progress throughout the study.

Name: _____ Class: _____

Class Topic: _____ My Topic: _____

Research Question: _____
_____

Notebook Due Dates: _____ _____ _____ _____

	DUE	COMPLETED	GRADE
1. Topic			
Presearch:	_____	_____	_____
Topic Choice:	_____	_____	_____
Concept Map:	_____	_____	_____
2. Goal Setting			
Research Question:	_____	_____	_____
Focus Questions:	_____	_____	_____
3. Research			
Notefact Cards:	_____	_____	_____
Source Cards:	_____	_____	_____
Glossary:	_____	_____	_____
4. Organizing			
Thesis Statement:	_____	_____	_____
Graphic Organizer:	_____	_____	_____
5. Goal Evaluation			
Objective Evaluation:	_____	_____	_____
Subjective Evaluation:	_____	_____	_____
6. Product			
Paper:	_____	_____	_____
Other:	_____	_____	_____
7. Presentation	_____	_____	_____

Presearch

Name: _____ Class: _____

Class Topic: _____

Teacher Question(s): _____

_____

_____

Read one selection about your area of interest. On the organizer below, record possible research topics, information about these topics, and ideas and questions you have.

Area of Interest:	
Possible Topic	**Information, Ideas, and Questions**

Proficient
Workpages

Developing the Research Topic

Name: _____

After finishing your presearch, examine what you have written and choose one topic as the focus of your research study. Write that topic in the oval below. Think of categories related to your topic as you build your concept map. Group what you know (prior knowledge) and what you want to find out (questions) around each category. You might want to develop your concept map electronically.

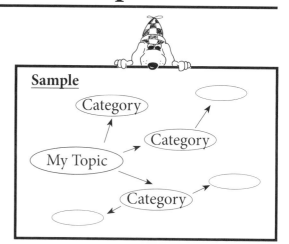

Sample

Concept Map

My Topic

Glossary of the Study

List the NEW words/concepts and their meanings that are key to helping others understand your topic.

_____   _____

_____   _____

                                 _____

_____   _____

                                 _____

_____   _____

                                 _____

_____   _____

                                 _____

_____   _____

                                 _____

_____   _____

                                 _____

_____   _____

                                 _____

_____   _____

                                 _____

**Proficient
Workpages**

Setting Research Goals

Name: _____

Developing the Research Question

A *Research Question* defines the issue or problem you will investigate. Using information from your Concept Map and the Teacher Question(s), formulate a *Research Question* that you find both worthy of exploring and of great interest.

Teacher Question(s): _____

_____

_____

My Research Question: _____

_____

_____

Focus Questions to Guide the Research

Write several *Focus Questions* that will help you find information relevant to your *Research Question*. Identify each with a capital letter in preparation for notefact cards.

My Focus Questions:

A. _____

_____

_____

_____

_____

_____

Sample

Class Unit: Native American Tribes   My Topic: Hopi Native Americans

Teacher Question: How does your tribe pass on its values and beliefs?

My Research Question: How are Hopi ceremonies and rituals used today to maintain ancient values and beliefs?

Focus Questions:

A What are their religious beliefs?
B. How are their origin stories transferred to current tribe members?
C. Etc....

Proficient Workpages

Setting Research Goals *(cont.)*

Teacher Goals

Listed below are the teacher-set goals for your study. They include the minimum number of notefacts, key vocabulary words (critical to understanding your topic), and resources you will use to gather your information.

Notefact Goal: ____   **Glossary Goal:** ____   **Resource Goal:** ____   **Primary Source Goal:** ____

Choosing Resources

Check at least 3 different types of resources you might use to make your study more interesting (PROVE). List possible sources of information for each type you checked.

☐ **P**ose a question: _____

☐ **R**ead: _____

☐ **O**bserve: _____

☐ **V**isit: _____

☐ **E**xamine: _____

Types of Resources to PROVE the Answers to Your Research Question

Pose a question: e-mail, interview, letter, survey, telephone, other: _____

Read: book (reference, text, non-fiction, fiction...), brochure, catalog, CD-ROM, field guide, magazine, newspaper, pamphlet, specialized dictionary, other: _____

Observe: art work, buildings, case & field study, diagrams, files, illustrations, movie, nature, photograph, speaker, TV, video, weather, workshop, other: _____

Visit: business, church, flea market, government agency, historical site, historical society, hospital, laboratory, meeting, museum, public/private/personal archives (attic, cellar, garage), sporting event, other: _____

Examine: advertisement, artifact, chart, collection, cook, document, experiment, graph, Internet (web site, newsgroup, forum, event calendar, mail list, search engine), map, microscope, poster, record/statistics, taste, other: _____

Key Terms

Primary Source - A first hand account of an event or an artifact created by the event where the author was present (newspaper, magazine article, diary, collection, photograph, manuscript, archival document...)

Secondary Source - A source that seeks to describe, explain, and interpret an event after it has happened when the author was not present (book, article, media production, any historical source or reproduction...)

Proficient Workpages

To Trust or Not to Trust
(Choosing valid sources)

No matter which type of resource you use – print, Internet, primary document, speaker, visual, etc. – it is important to evaluate the reliability of the information you find. These categories and questions should help you decide whether or not the resource will give you accurate information for your study.

1st Glance

1. Author (or the person delivering the information): Is s/he
   a. An expert in the field? (well-known, a researcher, connected to a reputable organization)
   b. Able to be contacted? (e-mail, snail mail address)
   c. An author of other articles? (listed in bibliography)

2. Publisher
   a. Well-known (a reputation for quality materials)
   b. If a website, who is the sponsor (page domain)?
      i. Edu (education), gov (government), net (network), and org (non-profit) tend to be the most reliable, and the bias should be evident from the sponsoring organization
      ii. Com (commercial – anyone can have one) should be examined more carefully.

3. Date (How current is it?)

4. Edition (The more revisions and reprintings, the more likely it is an accepted and reliable source.)

5. Reviews by an editor and/or a peer review group

6. Recommendations by a reliable source
   a. People: (librarian, teacher, researcher, scientist)
   b. Subject guide

In-Depth Examination

1. Intended audience (general or special group)

2. Bibliographies (useful to get to additional resources)
   a. Listing of scholarly references
   b. Links to reliable websites

3. Complete index, table of contents, and/or site map

4. Bias
   a. Clear, not hidden
   b. Opinions supported by strong evidence, not just the author's ideas
   c. Will the author gain personally from your use of the material?

5. Relevant information (backs up and adds to information from your other sources)

6. Title reflects the content

Taking Notefacts on Note Cards

Document all data-gathering sources (PROVE) and information on note cards.

Source Card Format

Fill out one source card for each resource. (See p. 145-146 for correct bibliographic format.)

   a. Put a number **1** in the upper right corner of the card to identify your first resource.

   b. Record if this is a primary source in the lower left corner of the card.

   c. Use a new card and number for each resource.

Notefact Card Format

   a. In the upper right corner, write **1** (for first resource) and A (for first *Focus Question*)

   b. Write your notefacts about that *Focus Question* from that resource on card(s) labeled **1-A**.

   c. Record the number of notefacts in the lower left corner of each card.

   d. If you go on to a new *Focus Question* from the same resource, start a new card identified with **1-B (1-C, 1-D)**.

   e. Follow steps a-d for additional resources, sequencing the numbers on each source card.

How to Write Notefacts

Record notefacts (short, true pieces of information) that help to answer one of your *Focus Questions*. Be sure to summarize findings from all research activities on notefact cards.

   a. Paraphrase information by writing facts in your own words. **Be careful not to plagiarize**.

   b. Keep notefacts short, but complete enough to make sense.

   c. Use quotation marks for direct quotes.

   d. Write the page number from text sources beside each notefact.

   e. Highlight key words and add them to your glossary (p. 139).

   f. Write your opinion(s) about the source and/or information in a different color.

Note Card Format

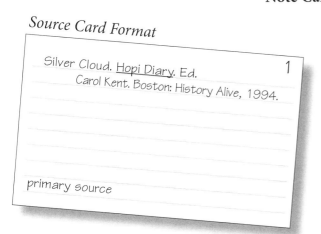

Source Card Format

Silver Cloud. Hopi Diary. Ed. Carol Kent. Boston: History Alive, 1994.   1

primary source

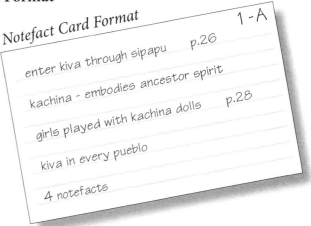

Notefact Card Format   1 - A

enter kiva through sipapu   p.26

kachina - embodies ancestor spirit

girls played with kachina dolls   p.28

kiva in every pueblo

4 notefacts

The Perils of Plagiarism

What is it?

PLAGIARISM IS using other authors' words and ideas in your writing without giving them credit.

Don't:

- cut and paste from on-line sources
- use another student's work as your own
- just change a few words from any source for your paper
- turn in a paper you wrote for another class

Why Shouldn't I?

Plagiarism is a serious offense and can lead to failing grades or suspension from school.

How Can I Avoid It? (To cite or not to cite)

1. Always develop a Working Bibliography and a Works Cited list.

2. Use quotation marks when you record the author's exact words.

3. Credit an author's new findings, interpretations, or point of view with in-text citations (name and page number within the text of your paper).

4. Common knowledge does not need in-text citations but must be written in your own words. Just list the source in your working bibliography.

Remember!

- Document all notefacts with source and page number.
- Vary your sources. It's hard to copy from a video, interview, experiment, museum display. . .
- Skim a text for relevant information before taking notefacts.
- After reading a passage, close the book and write what you learned in your own words.
- Photocopy an article, and highlight key words and phrases before writing notefacts.
- Notefacts shouldn't be complete sentences. Cross out unnecessary words.

Need More Help?

Try:

- *MLA Handbook for Writers of Research Papers*
- *The Research Paper Handbook*
- www.plagiarism.org
- www.psych.ufl.edu/~levy/plagiarz.htm
- Enter "plagiarism" into your favorite search engine

Just Say "No" to Plagiarism!

Proficient Workpages

Working Bibliography & Works Cited

Use the MLA documentation style below in developing your:
1. *Working bibliography* – a record of all sources used in your research.
2. *Works cited* – a list of all sources that you cite in the text of your paper.

Print Sources

BOOK: Author(s). <u>Title</u>. City of publication: Publisher, Date.

> Parker, Derek and Julia Barker. <u>Atlas of the Supernatural</u>. New York: Prentice Hall, 2000.

CHART, MAP, OR POSTER: <u>Title</u>. Map, chart, or poster. City of publication: Publisher, Date.

> <u>The Solar System</u>. Poster. Palo Alto: Dale Seymour Publications, 2007

ENCYCLOPEDIA AND REFERENCE BOOKS: Author(if given) or editor (ed.). "Title of article." <u>Title of book or publication</u>. edition year.

> Pope, Clifford. "Crocodile." <u>Encyclopedia Americana</u>. 2004 ed.

MAGAZINE: Author(s). "Title of article." <u>Name of magazine.</u> Date: Page numbers.

> Satchell, Michael. "To Save the Sequoias." <u>U.S News and World Report.</u> 7 Oct. 2006: 42-46.

NEWSPAPER: Author. "Title of article." <u>Name of Newspaper</u> [City if not part of name] Date, edition (if listed): Page(s).

> Murphy, Sean. "It Floats." <u>Rockingham News</u> [Exeter] 21 May 2009, late ed.: A1+.

PAMPHLET: Same style as book

Non-Print Sources

FIELD TRIP: Site. Location. Attending Group. Date.

> Longfellow-Evangeline State Commemorative Area. St. Martinville, LA. Grade 6, Maplewood Middle School. 13 March 2007.

INTERVIEW: Person interviewed. Type of interview (personal, telephone. . .). Date.

> Parsons, Mary. Telephone interview. 30 May 2008.

Proficient Workpages

Working Bibliography & Works Cited *(cont.)*

SOUND RECORDINGS: Artist. <u>Title of selection</u>. Medium (unless CD). Manufacturer, Date.

Kawamura, Masako. <u>Baratata-Batake</u>. Audiocassette. PWS Records, 1996.

SPEAKER: Speaker. "Title." Sponsoring organization. Location. Date.

Landry, Bob. "Acadiens." Maplewood 6th Grade Team. Maplewood Middle
School Auditorium, Sulphur, LA. 7 March 2009.

TELEVISION OR RADIO PROGRAM: "Title of episode or segment." Performer, narrator, director, or author. <u>Title of program</u>. Network. Call letters, City, Date(s).

"Secrets of Lost Empires." <u>Nova</u>. PBS. WGBH, Boston, 26 May 2007.

VIDEO: <u>Title</u>. Director or producer. Medium (unless film). Distributor, Date.

<u>Jurassic Park, The Lost World</u>. Dir. Stephen Speilberg. Videocassette. Century Fox, 1995.

Electronic Sources

CD-ROM: Author (if given). "Title of section." <u>Title of publication</u>. CD-ROM. edition, release, or version. City of publication: Publisher, Year.

"Whiskey Rebellion." <u>Microsoft Encarta</u>. CD-ROM. 2006 ed. New York: Funk & Wagnalls,
2006.

WEB PAGE: Author. "Title." Date of posting or latest update. Site sponsor or Internet site. Date of access <Electronic address or URL>.

Morse, Sarah. "Female Pedagogy." 25 May 2008. Morse Homepage. 3 August 2009
<http://www.morsefamily.com>.

ENTIRE WEB SITE: <u>Title of web site</u>. Editor (if given). Date of posting or latest update. Name of sponsoring organization. Date of access <Electronic address or URL>.

<u>Building Green Homes</u>. Harold House. 4 June 2008. Green Living. 30 April 2009
<http://greenliving.org>.

NOTE 1: You may use italics instead of the underlining used in the samples. Check with your teacher to see if there is a preference.

NOTE 2: For more detailed directions and complete listings, see <u>MLA Handbook for Writers of Research Papers</u> (Gibaldi 2009).

NOTE 3: You might want to use an electronic citation site. Be sure you have recorded all the necessary information while you are working on your notes. Two free sites are: Citation machine—<u>http://citationmachine.net</u> and Easy Bib—<u>www.easybib.com</u>

Proficient
Workpages

Organizing, Analyzing & Interpreting Data

Name: _____

Organizing

1. Set aside source cards for your bibliography.
2. Sort notefact cards by *Focus Questions*.

Analyzing

1. Thinking about your *Research Question* and the notefacts you've gathered, write a *Thesis Statement* you want to prove in your paper and/or product.

   Thesis Statement (sample):
   Religious practices in Hopi villages are the most important aspect of their culture.

   My Thesis Statement:

   _____

   _____

2. Separate information essential to proving your *Thesis Statement* from supplementary notefacts. If both types are on the same note card, circle or star the essential notefact(s). Count each group.

Essential notefacts: _____
Supplementary notefacts: _____

3. Using your essential notefacts, split *Focus Question* information into narrower categories if necessary.

   Choose:

   a. Color code, circle or underline, and make a key.

   b. Cut & paste - Identify each notefact with source number and *Focus Question* letter; place on chart/list.

4. Conduct further research if necessary to help prove your *Thesis Statement*.

5. Organize data on a(n)
   _____ outline,
   _____ graph/chart, and/or
   _____ graphic organizer (see p. 149).

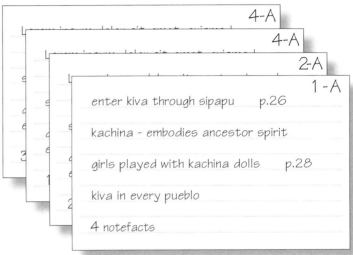

4-A
4-A
2-A
1-A
enter kiva through sipapu   p.26
kachina - embodies ancestor spirit
girls played with kachina dolls   p.28
kiva in every pueblo
4 notefacts

1-A
enter kiva through sipapu   p.26
★kachina - embodies ancestor spirit
★girls played with kachina dolls   p.28
★kiva in every pueblo
4 notefacts

Key
____ kiva
◯ kachina

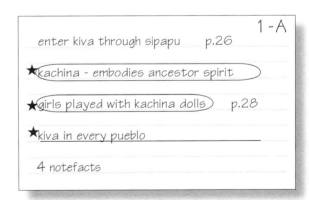

1-A
enter kiva through sipapu   p.26
★kachina - embodies ancestor spirit
★girls played with kachina dolls   p.28
★kiva in every pueblo
4 notefacts

Bar Graph

Proficient Workpages

Organizing, Analyzing & Interpreting Data *(cont.)*

Name: _____

Interpreting

Using your organized data, write an in-depth interpretation/conclusion about what you learned for each *Focus Question*. Begin each interpretation by writing the *Focus Question*. Use additional sheets of paper if necessary.

_____

_____

_____

_____

_____

_____

_____

_____

_____

_____

_____

_____

_____

_____

_____

_____

_____

_____

_____

_____

_____

_____

_____

_____

_____

_____

_____

Proficient Workpages

Sample Organizers

A. Graphic Organizer

Concept Map
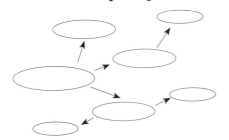

Venn Diagram
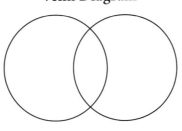

Hierarchical
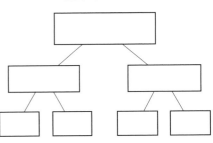

Cause and Effect
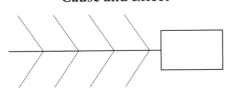

Cyclical
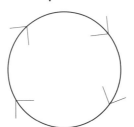

Timeline

Beginning
Date

Ending
Date

B. Graph

Bar
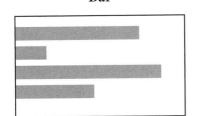

Pie
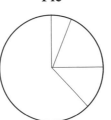

Line

C. Chart

Hierarchical

A	B	C	D

Matrix

	A	B	C	D
W				
X				
Y				
Z				

D. Outline

I.
    A.
       1.
       2.
    B.
II.
    A.
    B.
       1.
       2.

Evaluating Research Goals

Name: _____

Objective Evaluation

Fill in the information to evaluate the goals you set in Step 2.

	# OF RESOURCES	# OF PRIMARY SOURCES	# OF NOTEFACTS	# OF GLOSSARY ENTRIES	TYPE OF RESOURCES				
					P	R	O	V	E
REQUIRED									
ACHIEVED									

On the rubric, check the box that shows your level of accomplishment for each indicated criterion.

Proficient Workpages

IIM Research Rubric				
	LEVEL 1	LEVEL 2	LEVEL 3	LEVEL 4
Research Question	Unrelated to topic and unclear	Either related or clear	Related to topic Clear – Answerable Generalizable	Clear Relevant Answerable
Resources	Neither required # or types	Met requirement of # or types	Used all required # and types	Above requirement of # and types
Notefacts	0-1 of following: Met goal # Paraphrased – Short Related to *Focus Questions*	2-3 of following: Met goal # Paraphrased – Short Related to *Focus Questions*	Met goal # Paraphrased Related to *Focus Questions*	Above goal # Advanced vocabulary
Organizing	Unorganized Incomplete organizer	Use of required organizer Data weakly related to *Focus Questions*	Data organized and understandable Categories relate to *Focus Questions*	Use of more than required organizers *Focus Questions* split into subcategories
Conclusions/ Interpretations	Facts only	Weakly related to *Research Question* conclusions, not just facts	Gives reasons to support conclusions Related to *Research Question*	Synthesizes information to support conclusions

List 3 things you will do to improve your next research study.

1. _____

2. _____

3. _____

Evaluating Research Goals *(cont.)*

Subjective Evaluation

Describe in detail a major finding from your study. What is the impact of this finding? Use additional paper if necessary.

_____

_____

_____

_____

_____

_____

_____

_____

Explain what you learned about being a researcher and how that will help you in the future. Use additional paper if necessary.

_____

_____

_____

_____

_____

_____

_____

How would you grade yourself? _____

Why? _____

_____

_____

Teacher Response: _____

_____

_____

_____

Proficient Workpages

Writing a Research Paper

You have been assigned a research paper as an end product of your research. Your job is to explain the results of this study and to persuade the audience to accept your conclusions. Use the outline below to guide you through the WHAT and the HOW of a research paper. Your best support tools may be Lester's *The Research Paper Handbook,* Gibaldi's *MLA Handbook for Writers of Research Papers,* or the resource books made available by your teacher.

WHAT: The Parts of a Research Paper

Is your information clear and understandable? Interesting? Did you cite your sources and authorities? Did you proofread?

Title Page—with a title of 8-15 words

Introduction

> *Topic*—brief statement of the issues of the paper
>
> *Review of the Literature*—background information from other researchers
>
> *The Research Question*—the problem you researched
>
> *Thesis Statement*—what you will prove with your supporting study data

Body—development of the major issues of the study and supporting data (If data gathering included action research such as sampling, surveying, and experiments, you must include methods, materials, and results.)

Conclusion—your interpretation from research related to your thesis statement

Documentation—working bibliography (all sources used in research), in-text citations, and endnotes

HOW: The Writing Process

Thesis Statement—Develop a position statement from your *Research Question* that you will prove in your paper.

Outline—Make an outline for each section of your paper using facts, interpretations, and conclusions.

Rough Draft—From your outline, write a rough draft using data from your notefacts. Include in-text citations and direct quotes when appropriate.

Revise—Make necessary changes as you reread and rewrite each section of your paper.

Format—Use a standard guide to format the appearance of your paper with a title page, margins, spacing...

Edit—Check for correct writing mechanics and style.

Final Copy—Using all your revisions, formatting, and editing, complete the final copy of your paper to hand in to your teacher.

Proficient Workpages

Developing a Product

Name: _____

Audience

Circle audience types that would be interested in your research information.

Business   Competition   Community   Government   Organization   Parents
Professional   Publisher   School   Other: _____

Now write the exact audience for your presentation: _____

Product Choice

Considering your audience, choose a product type that will share your information with the greatest impact. Think of your strengths, available resources, and TIME.

Action: business venture, campaign, celebration, club, competition, dance, debate, demonstration, experiment, game, lesson, mentorship, performance, petition, recitation, simulation, speech, tour, _____

Collection: aquarium, art gallery, exhibit, learning center, list, portfolio, scrapbook, terrarium,
_____

Model: blueprint, costume, invention, musical instrument, origami, puppet, reproduction, scale model, _____

Technology: animation, computer program, database, photography, radio/TV broadcast, video/audio recording, web page, _____

Visual Representation: advertisement, artwork, brochure, bulletin board, bumper sticker, calendar, card, cartoon, collage, comic strip, flag, graph, graphic organizer, illustration, map, mural, photo essay, puzzle, scenery,
_____

Written Work: book, critique, diary, editorial, letter, magazine/newspaper article, musical composition, newsletter, pamphlet, poem, recipe, script, word puzzle,
_____

Proficient Workpages

Developing a Product *(cont.)*

Product Plan

Product choice:

_____

_____

Description of product:

_____

_____

_____

_____

Information shared from your research:

_____

_____

_____

_____

_____

Steps necessary to complete it:

_____

_____

_____

_____

Resources needed:

_____

_____

_____

_____

_____

How will you present this product?

recitation   letter writing   article   teaching   fair   workshop

conference   debate   simulation   other_____

Presentation of Research Findings

Name: _____

Product: _____

Audience: _____

Presentation mode: _____

_____

Presentation date/time: _____

Length of presentation: _____

Preparation for Presentation

People to contact: _____

Scheduling: _____

Presentation practice: _____

Set-up time: _____

Materials Needed

☐ 1. Notecards: _____

☐ 2. Visual Aids–list: _____

_____

☐ 3. Equipment: _____

_____

☐ 4. Handout—describe and attach copy: _____

Skills Needed

_____

_____

_____

_____

Help Needed

With skills: _____

At the presentation: _____

Research Product/Presentation Inventory

Name: _____

Keep a dated record of the products, presentations, and audiences you choose in Steps 6 & 7 of your research studies. Try to vary your choices.

Product Type
Action, Collection, Model, Technology, Visual Representation, Written Work

Presentation Mode
Article, Conference, Debate, Fair, Letter, Performance, Recitation, Simulation, Teaching

Audience Type
Business, Competition, Community, Government, Organization, Parents, Professional, Publisher, School

Date	Product Type	Product	Presentation Mode	Audience

Proficient Workpages

SECTION SIX

IIM - Proficient Level Sample Research Study

This sample IIM research study has been developed to help you understand the use of the IIM Unit Plan and the Student Workpages at the Proficient Level. This unit, Civil War, models a tenth grade study, and is being taught by both the English and History teachers. This student has mastered basic research skills and is capable of applying the higher level skills required at the Proficient Level.

The unit plan includes academic and study skills objectives based on state standards. There are "How to" skills that need to be taught as well as assessment strategies that relate directly to the objectives. The list of teacher resources was chosen to include both primary and secondary sources that would support and enhance the unit for this tenth grade class. Greta's resources are our creation. The two teachers have divided the work in the first 5 steps. For Product and Presentation, the English teacher is working on the research paper and the Social Studies teacher, on the museum display and presentation. All Student Workpages, including a research paper outline, have been included in this sample research study.

CONTENTS - SECTION SIX

Civil War Unit Plan...158
Student Booklet 163

Objectives, Skills, & Standards
IIM Unit Plan

Curriculum Unit: _Civil War_   Class: _History/English_

Dates: _1/30 - 3/5_   Time: _2nd period/5th period_

Process Used (circle):   _Basic Group_   _Basic Independent_   _Proficient Group_   (_Proficient Independent_)

Academic and Study Skills Objectives:

Students will:

Explore the factors that influenced the war

Identify the common elements of wars

Understand how war affects different segments of the population

Analyze how this war affected the future development of the USA

Learn vocabulary pertinent to the topic and discipline

Progress from writing a research report to a research paper

Write a research paper based on a thesis statement

Use correct bibliography format

Teacher Essential Question(s):

What are the common elements of war?

How are the different sides in a war impacted?

Analyze the effect of geography on a war.

"How To" Skills:

Teach students "How to":

Develop a research question and cite sources using MLA format

Paraphrase from a variety of resources

Locate and gather information from primary sources

Choose and use a graphic organizer appropriate to their study

Design a quality museum display

Standards Addressed:

Demonstrate an understanding of major topics from the Civil War (NH-Hist.-Standard 17)

Recognize relationships between primary and secondary sources (MA-Hist.-Standard 3)

Synthesize information from multiple sources (FL-LA-A.2.4.8)

Paraphrase/summarize text to recall, inform, or organize ideas (TX-Eng., LA Reading-8.10G)

Written reports: include appropriate facts and details, excluding extraneous and
    inappropriate information (VT-Comm.-1.8-e)

Develop a controlling idea that conveys a perspective on the subject (VT-Comm.-1.8-f)

Resources
IIM Unit Plan

Curriculum Unit: Civil War

List the resources you will use during the unit. Be sure to include some that are appropriate for the diverse learning needs and styles within your classroom.

Print: (book, computer, poster...)

Chang, I. *A Separate Battle: Women and the Civil War*. East Windsor Hill: Synergetics.

Emert, Phyllis Raybin. *Making a Statement with Song: Songs Reflecting the Social, Economic and Political Climate in American History*. Carlisle: Discovery Enterprises.

Forman, Stephen M. *Echoes of the Civil War: The Blue*. Carlisle: Discovery Enterprises.

Forman, Stephen M. *Echoes of the Civil War: The Grey*. Carlisle: Discovery Enterprises.

Johnson, David. *The Civil War*. Amawalk: Jackdaw Publications.

Non-Print: (field trip, video, experiment...)

Civil War Journal - Sets 1 & 2. Videocassette. Blacklick: Glencoe/McGraw Hill.

Jacksonburg Historical Society Museum. Jacksonburg. Grade 8, Jacksonburg Jr. High School. 19 Feb. 2009.

People: (speaker, parent volunteer, other teacher...)

Dr. Dixie Mason - State University history professor - speaker

Parent volunteer for help with field trips; Museum Day set up

Mr. Grantlee, school librarian

Preparatory Activities/Materials:

Student Booklet Pages: Sec. 5: p. 135-156

Transparencies: All student booklet pages

Other: Divide process steps between English and History

Schedule gymnasium for Museum Day

Immersion Activities:

Read Civil War textbook, Chapter 12

Attend Civil War Days battle reenactment - Jan. 30

Read current event articles about wars; locate war-torn countries on world map

Assessment
IIM Unit Plan

Curriculum Unit: _____

What *process skills* will you assess?

Ability to recognize common elements
  of war

Acquisition of new vocabulary

Using correct MLA bibliography format

Organizing data on a graphic organizer
  (Step 4)

Listening skills

Subjective evaluation of research process

How?

Informal check on class concept map

Use 10 key words in a Civil War diary entry

Grade source cards

Grade information as well as the usefulness
  of graphic organizer chosen

Test based on student presentations

Respond to student comments (Sec. 6: p. 179)

What *products* will you assess?

Research paper

Artifact and museum display

How?

Grade outline and final paper

Use rubric developed by class

7 Steps
IIM Unit Plan

Curriculum Unit: _____

List what you will do for each step of the process. Include unit activities, assessment strategies, and skills lessons. Identify ways you will differentiate for the diverse learning needs and styles of your students.

Step 1 Topic

Take class to Civil War battle reenactment at Jacksonburg Historical Society Civil War Days

Assign textbook chapter on Civil War

Work with class to make concept map on common elements of war

Develop class chart of student interest areas connected to class concept map

Take students to library to conduct presearch on interest area

Step 2 Goal Setting

Model development of research question using several student interest areas (skills lesson)

Set up class resource center with samples from each category of PROVE

Step 3 Research

Teach use of notefact and source cards using MLA format (skills lesson)

Show video to whole class for notefact gathering on individual topics

Help students choose one primary source for research

7 Steps
IIM Unit Plan *(cont.)*

STEP 4 Organizing

Guide students in developing thesis statement (skills lesson)

Model choice between essential and supplementary notefacts (skills lesson)

Guide students in choice of appropriate graphic organizer

STEP 5 Goal Evaluation

Assign diary entry with accurate use of at least 10 glossary words

Use 4 Corners (Kagan, Sec 8: p.5) cooperative learning technique for students to debrief their
progress as researchers, share new findings, and discuss ideas for museum display

Respond to student comments on *Evaluating Research Goals* (Sec. 6: p. 179)

STEP 6 Product

Develop class chart of possible artifacts and character costumes

Visit Civil War display at State Historical Museum and help students identify characteristics
of quality relics and displays

Develop rubric criteria with class for quality artifact and museum display

Set up computer page format for artifact description in Museum Guide Book

Use Sec. 6: p. 180 to teach students steps of writing a research paper (skills lesson)

STEP 7 Presentation

Provide adequate class time for practicing role playing and formal presentations

Guide students in use of *Fact Gathering for Presentations* (Sec. 2: p. 70) for recording
presentation facts to use as a study guide

Develop open-ended test allowing use of those individual study guides

Set up classroom for Museum Day, inviting appropriate classes, parents, . . .

IIM
Independent Investigation Method

IIM RESEARCH STUDY

Proficient Level

Name: *Greta Guard*

IIM Research Study Plan

This is your plan to keep records of each step of your IIM. Start with *Name, Class,* and *Class Topic.*
Add date goals set in class or by your teacher. Then fill in each section as you complete the step.
This allows you to stay on task and chart your progress throughout the study.

Name: *Greta Guard*   Class: *History/English*

Class Topic: *The Civil War*   My Topic: *Conditions in Civil*

Research Question: *What were the causes of the*   *War Prisons*
different levels of care in the Union and Confederate prisons?

Notebook Due Dates: *2/5 (Hist.)*   *2/12 (Eng.)*   *2/19 (Hist.)*   *3/5 (Eng.)*

	DUE	COMPLETED	GRADE
1. Topic *Hist./Eng.*			
Presearch:	*2/2*	*2/2*	
Topic Choice:	*2/3*	*2/3*	
Concept Map:	*2/4*	*2/4*	
2. Goal Setting *Hist.*			
Research Question:	*2/6*	*2/5*	*A*
Focus Questions:	*2/8*	*2/7*	
3. Research *Eng.*			
Notefact Cards:	*2/16*	*2/16*	*B+*
Source Cards:	*2/16*	*2/16*	*B+*
Glossary:	*2/16*	*2/16*	*A*
4. Organizing *Hist.*			
Thesis Statement:	*2/19*	*2/22*	*B+*
Graphic Organizer:	*2/19*	*2/22*	*B*
5. Goal Evaluation *Eng.*			
Objective Evaluation:	*2/19*	*2/22*	*B*
Subjective Evaluation:	*2/19*	*2/22*	
6. Product			
Paper: *Eng.*	*2/26*	*2/26*	*A–*
Other: *Museum display - Hist.*	*2/26*	*2/26*	*B*
7. Presentation – *Hist./Eng.*	*3/1*	*3/1*	*A*

Presearch

Name: *Greta Guard*   Class: *History/English*

Class Topic: *The Civil War*

Teacher Question(s): *What are the common elements of war?*

How are the different sides in a war impacted?

Analyze the effect of geography on a war.

Read one selection about your area of interest. On the organizer below, record possible research topics, information about these topics, and ideas and questions you have.

Area of Interest: *Civil War Prisons*	
Possible Topic	**Information, Ideas, and Questions**
Medical Care	*Were there hospitals?* *Unsanitary, few medicines, diseases killed lots* *Who treated prisoners?* *I could find out more about what diseases killed prisoners.*
Treatment of prisoners	*Cruel, killed for little reason, worse than regular convicts* *What food did they have?* *Did it depend on who was in charge? or who you were?*
Most famous prisons	*150 prisons:* *Andersonville, Libby - Confederate* *Camp Chase, Douglas, Morton - Union* *Some Union prisons in South* *So many prisons, it would be hard to compare*
Conditions	*What was it like in the different prisons?* *Lack of toilet facilities, crowded, hot buildings, outdoors with no shelter* *Is there is a correlation between the death rate at prisons and the conditions there?*

Developing the Research Topic

Name: _Greta Guard_

After finishing your presearch, examine what you have written and choose one topic as the focus of your research study. Write that topic in the oval below. Think of categories related to your topic as you build your concept map. Group what you know (prior knowledge) and what you want to find out (questions) around each category. You might want to develop your concept map electronically.

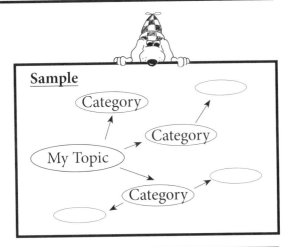

Sample

Concept Map

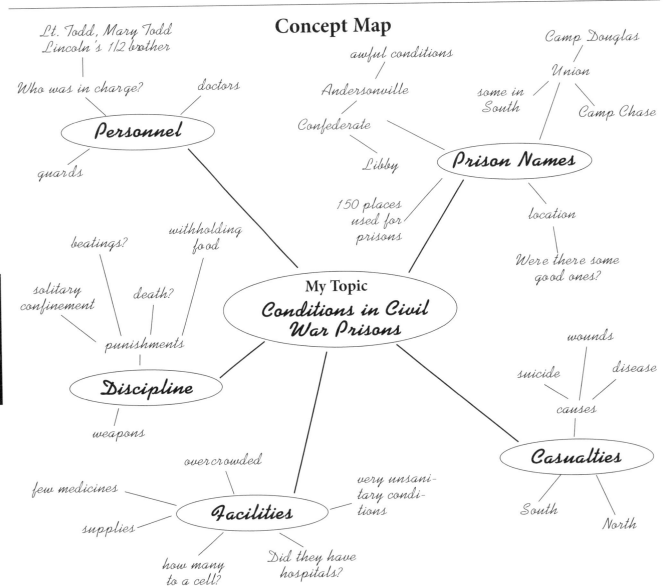

Lt. Todd, Mary Todd Lincoln's 1/2 brother

Who was in charge?　　_doctors_

Personnel

guards

awful conditions

Andersonville

Confederate

Libby

150 places used for prisons

Camp Douglas

Union

some in South

Camp Chase

Prison Names

location

Were there some good ones?

beatings?　　_withholding food_

solitary confinement　　_death?_

punishments

Discipline

weapons

My Topic
Conditions in Civil War Prisons

wounds

suicide　　_disease_

causes

Casualties

South　　_North_

overcrowded

few medicines

supplies

Facilities

very unsanitary conditions

how many to a cell?　　_Did they have hospitals?_

Setting Research Goals

Name: *Greta Guard*

Developing the Research Question

A *Research Question* defines the issue or problem you will investigate. Using information from your Concept Map and the Teacher Question(s), formulate a *Research Question* that you find both worthy of exploring and of great interest.

Teacher Question(s):   *What are the common elements of war? How are the different sides in a war impacted? Analyze the effect of geography on a war.*

My Research Question: *What were the causes for the different levels of care in the Confederate and Union prisons?*

Focus Questions to Guide the Research

Write several *Focus Questions* that will help you find information relevant to your *Research Question*. Identify each with a capital letter in preparation for notefact cards.

My Focus Questions:

A. *What were the names & locations of the largest prisons?*
B. *What were the prisoner casualty rates in the Confederate & Union prisons?*
C. *What medical provisions were made for prisoners with wounds and disease?*
D. *Describe the relationship between the sanitary conditions and the prison population.*
E. *How did political and human factors affect prisoner care?*

Sample

Class Unit: Native American Tribes   My Topic: Hopi Native Americans

Teacher Question: How does your tribe pass on its values and beliefs?

My Research Question: *How are Hopi ceremonies and rituals used today to maintain ancient values and beliefs?*

Focus Questions:

A. *What are their religious beliefs?*
B. *How are their origin stories transferred to current tribe members?*
C. *Etc....*

Setting Research Goals *(cont.)*

Teacher Goals

Listed below are the teacher-set goals for your study. They include the minimum number of note-facts, key vocabulary words (critical to understanding your topic), and resources you will use to gather your information.

Notefact Goal: _65_   **Glossary Goal:** _10_   **Resource Goal:** _4_   **Primary Source Goal:** _1_

Choosing Resources

Check at least 3 different types of resources you might use to make your study more interesting (PROVE). List possible sources of informatjion for each type you checked.

☐ **P**ose a question: *Civil War expert*

☑ **R**ead: *magazines, books, Civil War letters, Civil War news articles*

☑ **O**bserve: *video, pictures*

☑ **V**isit: *historical society, Gettysburg*

☐ **E**xamine: *Internet web sites*

Types of Resources to PROVE the Answers to Your Research Question

Pose a question: e-mail, interview, letter, survey, telephone, other: _____

Read: book (reference, text, non-fiction, fiction...), brochure, catalog, CD-ROM, field guide, magazine, newspaper, pamphlet, specialized dictionary, other: _____

Observe: art work, buildings, case & field study, diagrams, files, illustrations, movie, nature, photograph, speaker, TV, video, weather, workshop, other: _____

Visit: business, church, flea market, government agency, historical site, historical society, hospital, laboratory, meeting, museum, public/private/personal archives (attic, cellar, garage), sporting event, other: _____

Examine: advertisement, artifact, chart, collection, cook, document, experiment, graph, Internet (web site, newsgroup, forum, event calendar, mail list, search engine), map, microscope, poster, record/statistics, taste, other: _____

Key Terms

Primary Source - A first hand account of an event or an artifact created by the event where the author was present (newspaper, magazine article, diary, collection, photograph, manuscript, archival document...)

Secondary Source - A source that seeks to describe, explain, and interpret an event after it has happened when the author was not present (book, article, media production, any historical source or reproduction...)

To Trust or Not to Trust
(Choosing valid sources)

No matter which type of resource you use – print, Internet, primary document, speaker, visual, etc. – it is important to evaluate the reliability of the information you find. These categories and questions should help you decide whether or not the resource will give you accurate information for your study.

1st Glance

1. Author (or the person delivering the information): Is s/he
   a. An expert in the field? (well-known, a researcher, connected to a reputable organization)
   b. Able to be contacted? (e-mail, snail mail address)
   c. An author of other articles? (listed in bibliography)

2. Publisher
   a. Well-known (a reputation for quality materials)
   b. If a website, who is the sponsor (page domain)?
      i. Edu (education), gov (government), net (network), and org (non-profit) tend to be the most reliable, and the bias should be evident from the sponsoring organization
      ii. Com (commercial – anyone can have one) should be examined more carefully.

3. Date (How current is it?)

4. Edition (The more revisions and reprintings, the more likely it is an accepted and reliable source.)

5. Reviews by an editor and/or a peer review group

6. Recommendations by a reliable source
   a. People (librarian, teacher, researcher, scientist)
   b. Subject guide

In-Depth Examination

1. Intended audience (general or special group)

2. Bibliographies (useful to get to additional resources)
   a. Listing of scholarly references
   b. Links to reliable websites

3. Complete index, table of contents, and/or site map

4. Bias
   a. Clear, not hidden
   b. Opinions supported by strong evidence, not just the author's ideas
   c. Will the author gain personally from your use of the material?

5. Relevant information (backs up and adds to information from your other sources)

6. Title reflects the content

Taking Notefacts on Note Cards

Document all data-gathering sources (PROVE) and information on note cards.

Source Card Format

Fill out one source card for each resource. (See p. 145-146 for correct bibliographic format.)

a. Put a number **1** in the upper right corner of the card to identify your first resource.

b. Record if this is a primary source in the lower left corner of the card.

c. Use a new card and number for each resource.

Notefact Card Format

a. In the upper right corner, write **1** (for first resource) and A (for first *Focus Question*)

b. Write your notefacts about that *Focus Question* from that resource on card(s) labeled **1-A**.

c. Record the number of notefacts in the lower left corner of each card.

d. If you go on to a new *Focus Question* from the same resource, start a new card identified with **1-B (1-C, 1-D)**.

e. Follow steps a-d for additional resources, sequencing the numbers on each source card.

How to Write Notefacts

Record notefacts (short, true pieces of information) that help to answer one of your *Focus Questions*. Be sure to summarize findings from all research activities on notefact cards.

a. Paraphrase information by writing facts in your own words. **Be careful not to plagiarize**.

b. Keep notefacts short, but complete enough to make sense.

c. Use quotation marks for direct quotes.

d. Write the page number from text sources beside each notefact.

e. Highlight key words and add them to your glossary (p. 139).

f. Write your opinion(s) about the source and/or information in a different color.

Note Card Format

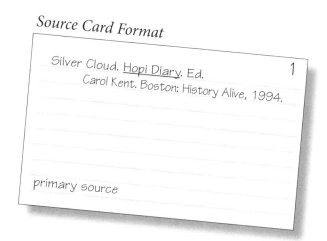

Source Card Format

Silver Cloud. <u>Hopi Diary</u>. Ed.
Carol Kent. Boston: History Alive, 1994.   1

primary source

Notefact Card Format   1-A

enter kiva through sipapu   p.26

kachina - embodies ancestor spirit

girls played with kachina dolls   p.28

kiva in every pueblo

4 notefacts

Glossary of the Study

List the NEW words/concepts and their meanings that are key to helping others understand your topic.

dysentery	*infectious disease characterized by severe diarrhea*
typhoid fever	*bacterial infection with high fever, rashes, headaches - carried by body lice*
vermin	*small, common, harmful animals - lice/fleas - difficult to control*
deadline	*wooden railing - anyone who crossed was shot by sentries in pigeon roost*
pigeon roost	*boxes for sentries on top of stockade fence*
pantaloons	*type of loose pants worn by soldiers*
desiccated vegetables	*dried vegetables given to prisoners*
crowd poisoning	*diseases/death caused by overcrowded conditions*
emaciated	*to waste away physically from sickness or lack of food*
dog tent	*term for prison tent only big enough for dog - housed 2-3 men*
cartel	*system of prisoner exchange*

Source 1

Card 1-A (marked 6)

Andersonville - GA - Conf. p. 42

20 people in Ander. bef. prison built p. 42

Libby - VA - Conf. p. 46

Camp Chase - OH - Union p. 82

Camp Morton - IN - Union p. 82

Elmira - NY - Union - Andersonville

of N p. 97

Card 1-D (marked 4)

Confederate

floors covered w/human filth p. 231

polluted water, food decaying in

sun p. 232

vermin, no shelter from heat or

cold p. 233

Union

medical examiner report - Elmira - good

sanitary conditions p. 272

Card 1 (marked 1)

Farley, Joseph. Famous Prisons of

the Civil War. New York: Pentium

Publishing Co., 1993.

Card 1-B (marked 4)

prison death rates

Union - 12% - 26,436 of 220,000 p. 101

Conf. - 8.3% - 22,570 of 270,000 p. 102

Andersonville - 30% p. 103

Source 2

2-D

Camp Douglas - Chicago
12,000 in stables and barracks for 8,000
largest Confed. burial ground
   outside South
Andersonville - built for 10,000
   peak # - 33,000

4

2-C

no medicine
diseases - typhoid, dysentery, malaria
Elmira - 1 surgeon, 11 assistants
" much of the sickness is attributed to
   crowd poisoning " (Elmira Medical Insp.)
new prisoners entered very ill
overcrowded hosp./stayed in barracks
stayed in bed after well cuz no clothes

7

2

Captives of War. CD-Rom. Palo Alto:
   Sunbelt Software, Inc., 1996.

2-B

Union prison - 12% - 25,976 of
   214,000
Conf. prisons - 15.5% - 30,218
   of 211,000

2

Source 3

Proficient Sample Study

3-A

Andersonville - good location near
fresh water, deep south, on RR line
harshest Union prisons - Elmira, Johnson's
Is. - Lake Erie, Camp Douglas

2

3-B

Capt. Wirz - heartless, abusive,

supplies sent from N to S not delivered

hospitals as corrupt as whole prison

guards - old men & boys

4

3

"Civil War Letters". 6 May 1997.
Gettysburg Historical
Society. 9 Feb. 1999.
<http://www.civilwarletters.com>.

Primary source

3-C

more died from disease than killed
in battle
plagues of smallpox
lack of surgical tools
use of herbs
Andersonville - no doctors

5

Organizing, Analyzing & Interpreting Data

Name: _Greta Guard_

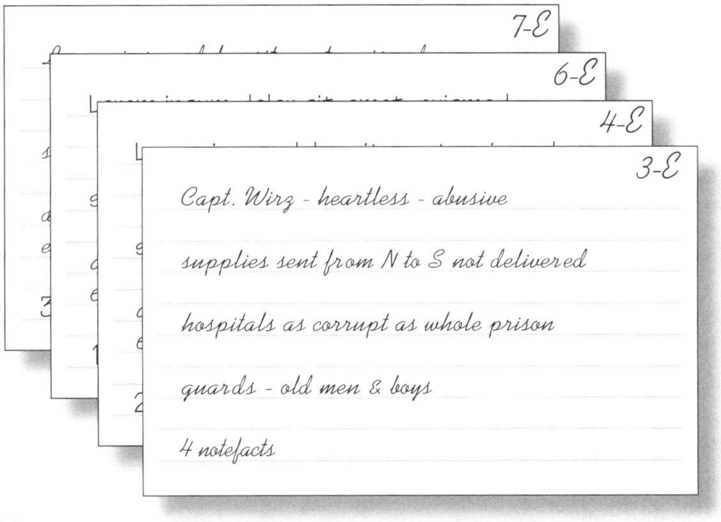

Organizing

1. Set aside source cards for your bibliography.
2. Sort notefact cards by *Focus Questions*.

Analyzing

1. Thinking about your *Research Question* and the notefacts you've gathered, write a *Thesis Statement* you want to prove in your paper and/or product.

   Thesis Statement (sample):
   Religious practices in Hopi villages are the most important aspect of their culture.

   My Thesis Statement: *Of all the factors affecting the conditions of Civil War prisoners, the human factor was the most significant*

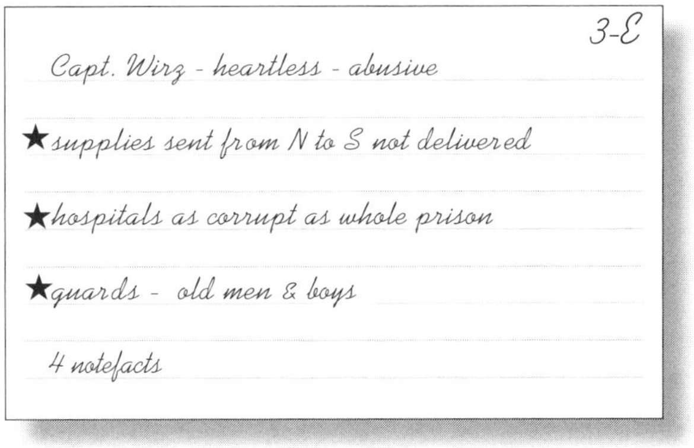

2. Separate information essential to proving your *Thesis Statement* from supplementary notefacts. If both types are on the same note card, circle or star the essential notefact(s). Count each group.

Essential notefacts: _42_
Supplementary notefacts: _26_

3. Using your essential notefacts, split *Focus Question* information into narrower categories if necessary.

   Choose:

   a. Color code, circle or underline, and make a key.

   b. Cut & paste - Identify each notefact with source number and *Focus Question* letter; place on chart/list.

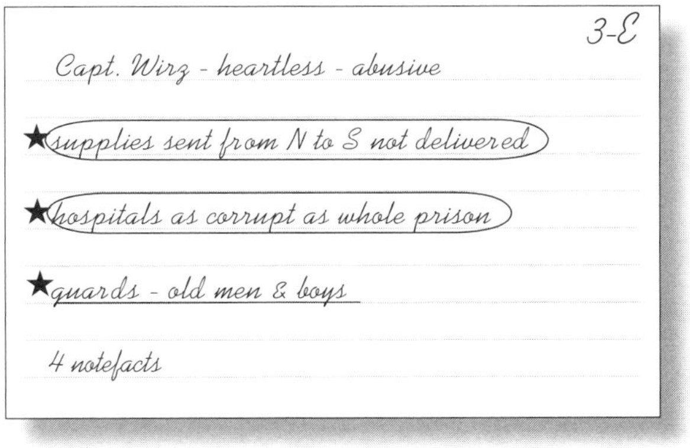

4. Conduct further research if necessary to help prove your *Thesis Statement*.

I need more information on Focus Question B. I have conflicting data on Confederate casualty rates.

Note cards (top right):

7-E

6-E

4-E

3-E
Capt. Wirz - heartless - abusive
supplies sent from N to S not delivered
hospitals as corrupt as whole prison
guards - old men & boys
4 notefacts

Note card (middle right):

3-E
Capt. Wirz - heartless - abusive
★supplies sent from N to S not delivered
★hospitals as corrupt as whole prison
★guards - old men & boys
4 notefacts

Key:
— Human
◯ Political

Note card (bottom right):

3-E
Capt. Wirz - heartless - abusive
★(supplies sent from N to S not delivered)
★(hospitals as corrupt as whole prison)
★guards - old men & boys
4 notefacts

Organizing, Analyzing & Interpreting Data *(cont.)*

Proficient Sample Study

5. Organize data on a(n) _____ outline, _____ graph/chart, and/or _____ ✔ graphic organizer (see Sec. 5: p. 149).

SOUTH

Human Factors
— deadline
— guards = old men & boys
— civilian aid denied

Casualty Rate
— 8.3%
— 15.5%
— 14.9%

Political Factors
— blocked delivery of N. supplies
— Rep. Foote = law for good treatment

Anderson-ville, GA
— Wirz = superintendent.
— good location
— fresh water
— RR line.
— 30% casualty rate

Libby, VA
Lt. Todd

Sanitary Conditions
no sanitizing

Medical Care
used herbs

COMMON

Medical Care
— lack of supplies, clothing, doctors, & knowledge
— no facilities
— prisoners entered ill

Sanitary Conditions
— polluted water, mud, vermin, crowd poisoning
— more died from disease than on battlefield

Political Factors
— retaliation treatment
— moved prisoners during daylight

Human Factors
— harsh commanders
— civilians offered aid
— officers primary cause of conditions

NORTH

Human Factor
withheld food

Political Factors
— officer prisoners = special treatment.
— 600 officers mistreated.

Elmira, NY
— good water.
— largest Conf. burial ground outside South
— Andersonville of North

Camp Douglas, IL
— damp
— muddy

Sanitary Conditions
Union Med.
Examiner report = some toilets, ventilation, sanitizing

Casualty Rate
12%

Medical Care
Union Med
Examiner report at Elmira = some doctors & facilities

Organizing, Analyzing & Interpreting Data *(cont.)*

Name: *Greta Guard*

Interpreting

Using your organized data, write an in-depth interpretation/conclusion about what you learned for each *Focus Question*. Begin each interpretation by writing the *Focus Question*. Use additional sheets of paper if necessary.

A. What were the names and locations of the largest prisons?

    The prisons I used for my study were 4 of the largest and best known prisons. They were good examples of the conditions in both the North: Elmira - NY; Camp Douglas, IL; and the South: Andersonville - GA; Libby - VA. The sizes and locations seemed to determine . . .

B. What were casualty rates in the Union and Confederate prisons?

    It appears from some sources that the casualty rates for both the North and South were quite similar - 12-15%. However, the data for the Confederate prisons was inconsistent - 8.3 to 15.5% - showing the inaccuracy of data collection at the time. Also, it was not clear...

C. What medical provisions were made for prisoners with wounds and diseases?

    Considering the lack of medical supplies, facilities, personnel, and knowledge of infection and disease, it was impossible to treat sick and wounded who entered the prison. Disease was spread by . . .

D. Describe the relationship between sanitary conditions and prison population.

    Many prisons may have had better conditions if the overcrowding had not . . .

E. What were the political and human factors affecting prisoner care?

    The terrible conditions at the Confederate and Union prisons were caused by both political and human factors. Among the political . . .

**Proficient
Sample Study**

Evaluating Research Goals

Name: *Greta Guard*

Objective Evaluation

Fill in the information to evaluate the goals you set in Step 2.

	# OF RESOURCES	# OF PRIMARY SOURCES	# OF NOTEFACTS	# OF GLOSSARY ENTRIES	TYPE OF RESOURCES				
					P	R	O	V	E
REQUIRED	*4*	*1*	*60*	*10*		✔	✔	✔	
ACHIEVED	*5*	*1*	*68*	*11*		✔	✔		✔

On the rubric, check the box that shows your level of accomplishment for each indicated criterion.

IIM Research Rubric

	LEVEL 1	LEVEL 2	LEVEL 3	LEVEL 4
Research Question	Unrelated to topic and unclear	Either related or clear	Related to topic Clear – Answerable Generalizable ✔	Clear Relevant Answerable
Resources	Neither required # or types	Met requirement of # or types ✔	Used all required # and types	Above requirement of # and types
Notefacts	0-1 of following: Met goal # Paraphrased – Short Related to *Focus Questions*	2-3 of following: Met goal # Paraphrased – Short Related to *Focus Questions*	Met goal # Paraphrased Related to *Focus Questions*	Above goal # Advanced vocabulary ✔
Organizing	Unorganized Incomplete organizer	Use of required organizer Data weakly related to *Focus Questions*	Data organized and understandable Categories relate to *Focus Questions* ✔	Use of more than required organizers *Focus Questions* split into subcategories
Conclusions/ Interpretations	Facts only	Weakly related to *Research Question* conclusions, not just facts	Gives reasons to support conclusions Related to *Research Question*	Synthesizes information to support conclusions ✔

List 3 things you will do to improve your next research study.

1. *Use all the required types of resources.*

2. *Gather more information that relates specifically to my Focus Questions.*

3. *Organize my data using statistics.*

Evaluating Research Goals *(cont.)*

Subjective Evaluation

Describe in detail a major finding from your study. What is the impact of this finding? Use additional paper if necessary.

As I read my Research Question, I realized I was saying that there really was a difference in the conditions and treatment of prisoners in the Confederate and Union prisons. Then, as I analyzed my Focus Questions, I saw that the differences were caused more by political, human, and geographic factors than whether the prison was run by the Union or the Confederacy. Politicians on both sides...

Explain what you learned about being a researcher and how that will help you in the future. Use additional paper if necessary.

I learned it is important to check who the author is and if the information might be biased. This is especially true in primary sources and on the Internet. In choosing sources for future studies, I should...

How would you grade yourself?_____*B*_____

Why? *I didn't use all the required types of resources, but I went over my notefact goal. The analysis of my data was...*

Teacher Response: Your use of primary sources added greatly to the depth of your conclusions. Your growth as a researcher...

Proficient Sample Study

Writing a Research Paper

You have been assigned a research paper as an end product of your research. Your job is to explain the results of this study and to persuade the audience to accept your conclusions. Use the outline below to guide you through the WHAT and the HOW of a research paper. Your best support tools may be Lester's *The Research Paper Handbook*, Gibaldi's *MLA Handbook for Writers of Research Papers*, or the resource books made available by your teacher.

Is your information clear and understandable? Interesting? Did you cite your sources and authorities? Did you proofread?

WHAT: The Parts of a Research Paper

Title Page—with a title of 8-15 words

Introduction

Topic—brief statement of the issues of the paper

Review of the Literature—background information from other researchers

The Research Question—the problem you researched

Thesis Statement—what you will prove with your supporting study data

Body—development of the major issues of the study and supporting data (If data gathering included action research such as sampling, surveying, and experiments, you must include methods, materials, and results.)

Conclusion—your interpretation from research related to your thesis statement

Documentation—working bibliography (all sources used in research), in-text citations, and endnotes

HOW: The Writing Process

Thesis Statement—Develop a position statement from your *Research Question* that you will prove in your paper.

Outline—Make an outline for each section of your paper using facts, interpretations, and conclusions.

Rough Draft—From your outline, write a rough draft using data from your notefacts. Include in-text citations and direct quotes when appropriate.

Revise—Make necessary changes as you reread and rewrite each section of your paper.

Format—Use a standard guide to format the appearance of your paper with a title page, margins, spacing...

Edit—Check for correct writing mechanics and style.

Final Copy—Using all your revisions, formatting, and editing, complete the final copy of your paper to hand in to your teacher.

Writing a Research Paper (cont.)

Outline

I. Introduction
   A. Topic - Conditions in Civil War Prisons
   B. Background Information
      1. Prison names/numbers
      2. Casualty rates/causes
      3. Medical care
      4. Sanitary conditions
   C. Research Question - What were the causes of the different levels of care in the Union and Confederate prisons?
   D. Thesis Statement: Of the political, geographic, and human factors affecting the condition of Civil War prisoners, the human factor was the most significant.

II. Body
   A. Human Factors
      1. Commanders
         a. Andersonville
            1) Wirz, Winder - cruelest
            2) made stay out in worst conditions
         b. Libby
            1) Lt. Todd
            2) shot prisoners for breathing
         c. Douglas
            1) withheld food
            2) suffocation building
         d. Elmira
            1) Andersonville of North
            2) torture areas
      2. Guards
         a. young boys, old men
         b. lack of training
         c. fearful-shot for no reason-deadline
         d. stole from prisoners
      3. Prison Population
         a. rank
            1) officers better treatment
            2) only enlisted men released during war
         b. race = factor in level of care
         c. population
            1) crowd poisoning
            2) sanitary conditions
            3) arrived in weakened state
            4) disease killed 3x more than battle wounds
   B. Geographic
      1. Features of good location
         a. water
         b. flat land
         c. closeness to supply lines
         d. climate
      2. Andersonville
         a. met all conditions for good location
         b. developed worst conditions
      3. Douglas - poor drainage area
   C. Political
      1. Lack of supplies
      2. No agreed upon system of prisoner exchange
      3. Politicians advocated both good and bad treatment
         a. starvation policy before exchanging prisoners
         b. retaliation towards prisoners on both sides
         c. Foote (S. Rep.) proposed law to improve conditions

III. Conclusion
   A. Human factors most significant
      1. Overcrowding
      2. Inhumanity of prison personnel and politicians
      3. . . .

Proficient Sample Study

Developing a Product

Name: *Greta Guard*

Audience

Circle audience types that would be interested in your research information.

Business Competition (Community) Government Organization (Parents)
Professional (Publisher) (School) Other: _____

Now write the exact audience for your presentation: *School/Community*

Product Choice

Considering your audience, choose a product type that will share your information with the greatest impact. Think of your strengths, available resources, and TIME.

Action: business venture, campaign, celebration, club, competition, dance, debate, demonstration, experiment, game, lesson, mentorship, performance, petition, recitation, simulation, speech, tour, _____

Collection: aquarium, art gallery, exhibit, learning center, list, portfolio, scrapbook, terrarium, _____

Model: blueprint, (costume) invention, (musical instrument) origami, puppet, reproduction, scale model, _____

Technology: animation, computer program, database, photography, radio/TV broadcast, video/ (audio recording) web page, _____

Visual Representation: advertisement, artwork, brochure, bulletin board, bumper sticker, calendar, card, cartoon, collage, comic strip, flag, graph, graphic organizer, illustration, map, mural, photo essay, puzzle, scenery, *backdrop* _____

Written Work: book, critique, diary, editorial, letter, magazine/newspaper article, (musical composition) newsletter, pamphlet, poem, recipe, script, word puzzle, _____

Developing a Product *(cont.)*

Product Plan

Product choice:

Song, costume, instrument, backdrop

Description of product:

Song - tune "Tenting Tonight", words - describing prison conditions

Costume - rags

Instrument - my sister's wooden recorder

Backdrop - paintings of dog tent, campfire, deadline w/ pigeon roost

Information shared from your research:

Bored prisoners sang songs to keep from going crazy.

I'll take info from notefacts in song words to show prison name,

    conditions, and longing for home.

Instrument, costume, and backdrop will show actual things from the time

period and prison life.

Steps necessary to complete it:

1. Get music from music teacher. 2. Write words. 3. Have Suzanne play

tune while I sing and tape this. 4. Make tattered costume from Dad's

old chino pants & denim shirt. 5. Paint backdrop pictures of dog tent,

campfire, and deadline w/ pigeon roost.

Resources needed:

Old pants and shirt, rags, recorder, tape recorder, butcher paper, paint

and brushes, sheet music of "Tenting Tonight"

How will you present this product?

    recitation   letter writing   article   teaching   (fair)   workshop

    conference   debate   simulation   other_____

Presentation of Research Findings

Name: *Greta Guard*

Product: *Museum display — song, backdrop, prisoner clothing, recorder*
Audience: *School and community*
Presentation mode: *Fair: Play song and talk to people as ragged, sickly soldier living in dog tent. People can sing along if they want to.*
Presentation date/time: *March 5, 6:00-8:00 pm*
Length of presentation: *Fair will be 2 hrs long; my song on tape recorder —2 min.*

Preparation for Presentation

People to contact: *Mr. Clean for set-up*

Scheduling:

Presentation practice: *Ms. Reb will let us practice in class; also at home*

Set-up time: *1/2 hr.*

Materials Needed

[X] 1. Notecards: *With some facts from my research*
[X] 2. Visual Aids–list: *Backdrop showing dog tent and campfire*

[X] 3. Equipment: *Tape recorder to play music, recorder*

[X] 4. Handout—describe and attach copy: *Copy of the song*

Skills Needed

Writing song to match the music

Help Needed

With skills: *Writing song — Ms. Melody; Painting on backdrop — Sarah*
At the presentation: *Help hanging backdrop — Mr. Clean*

Assessment
Criteria List Rubric: *(Step or Skill)*

Name(s): Greta Guard

Topic: Conditions in Civil War Prisons   Date: 2/26/99

Name of Peer Evaluator: Carl Convict

For the Teacher: *Create with class or assign criteria for quality work. If you decide to give a grade, use the total possible points to decide on a range for letter grades.*

CRITERIA	STUDENT OR PEER	TEACHER	COMMENT
Shows knowledge of topic	4	4	Lots of information
Organized	3	2	Plan more time for set-up
Interesting	4	3	
Realistic artifact	2	2	There were no computers for typing
Quality visuals	4	4	Realistic visuals on backdrop
Creative	4	3	
TOTAL	19	18	= 37

Grading

A = 43 - 48   D = 25 - 30

B = 37 - 42   **Not**

C = 31 - 36   **Yet** = Below 24

Final Grade = ___B___

Ratings

1 = Just Beginning   3 = Made It

2 = Moving Up   4 = Over the Top

Research Product/Presentation Inventory

Name: _Greta Guard_

Keep a dated record of the products, presentations, and audiences you
choose in Steps 6 & 7 of your research studies. Try to vary your choices.

> **Product Type**
> Action, Collection, Model, Technology, Visual Representation, Written Work
>
> **Presentation Mode**
> Article, Conference, Debate, Fair, Letter, Performance, Recitation,
> Simulation, Teaching
>
> **Audience Type**
> Business, Competition, Community, Government, Organization, Parents,
> Professional, Publisher, School

Proficient Sample Study

Date	Product Type	Product	Presentation Mode	Audience
10/97	Action	Dance	Performance	7th grade classes
4/98	Collection	Interest center	Teaching	4th grade buddies
2/26/99	Written	Research paper		Teacher
2/26/99	Model, Written, Visual	Costume, Song Backdrop	Fair	School Community

SECTION SEVEN

IIM Assessment

This section provides a variety of tools for diagnosing and improving skills, and measuring accomplishments as students go through the 7 steps of IIM. Some are designed to debrief the entire process; others, to assess one step or skill. There are journals for both the teacher and students, check lists, conference logs, and rubrics. We have also included examples of ways teachers have used the forms in their IIM units. Whatever you choose, be sure you identify what you are assessing: process, product, or content. Then make this clear to your students.

Many of the forms can be customized, saved for future use, and printed from the IIM Companion CD.

CONTENTS - SECTION SEVEN

IIM Assessment Forms...189
Samples of the Forms...203

Assessment

Assessment

IIM

Assessment Forms

OVERVIEW

These are forms to use with the full IIM process, individual steps, or specific skills. You may modify them to address your students' grade and skill levels as well as your own specific academic and grading needs.

You can design your forms electronically on the IIM Companion CD by adding your criteria in selected areas.

Assessment
IIM Teacher Reflection Journal

Curriculum Unit: _____   Class: _____

Write thoughts, ideas, problems, and suggestions about each step of IIM. This could be about your teaching, individual students, or specific lessons.

STEP 1 Topic

STEP 2 Goal Setting

STEP 3 Research

STEP 4 Organizing

STEP 5 Goal Evaluation

STEP 6 Product

STEP 7 Presentation

Assessment
IIM Student Reflection Journal

Name: _____

Unit: _____ My Topic: _____

Reflect on each step of IIM. Look back at your student booklet pages to help you.

STEP 1 Topic   *Date completed:_____*

What I did well: _____

_____

What I will work on next time: _____

_____

Teacher comments: _____

_____

_____

STEP 2 Goal Setting   *Date completed:_____*

What I did well: _____

_____

What I will work on next time: _____

_____

Teacher comments: _____

_____

_____

STEP 3 Research   *Date completed:_____*

What I did well: _____

_____

What I will work on next time: _____

_____

Teacher comments: _____

_____

_____

Assessment

IIM Student Reflection Journal *(cont.)*

STEP 4 Organizing   *Date completed:*_____

What I did well: _____

_____

What I will work on next time: _____

_____

Teacher comments: _____

_____

STEP 5 Goal Evaluation   *Date completed:*_____

What I did well: _____

_____

What I will work on next time: _____

_____

Teacher comments: _____

_____

STEP 6 Product   *Date completed:*_____

What I did well: _____

_____

What I will work on next time: _____

_____

Teacher comments: _____

_____

STEP 7 Presentation   *Date completed:*_____

What I did well: _____

_____

What I will work on next time: _____

_____

Teacher comments: _____

_____

Assessment

Assessment
IIM Observation Checklist

Name: _____

Topic: _____

┌─────────────────────────────────────┐
│ **Ratings** │
│ **1** = Just Beginning **3** = Made It │
│ **2** = Moving Up   **4** = Over the Top │
└─────────────────────────────────────┘

		STUDENT RATING	TEACHER RATING
STEP 1 Topic	Concept Map:	_____	_____
	_____	_____	_____
STEP 2 Goal Setting	Questions:	_____	_____
	_____	_____	_____
STEP 3 Research	Notefacts		
	Not plagiarized:	_____	_____
	Enough information:	_____	_____
	Short:	_____	_____
	Related to Goal Setting questions:	_____	_____
	_____	_____	_____
STEP 4 Organizing	Category choices:	_____	_____
	Notefacts in correct categories:	_____	_____
	_____	_____	_____
STEP 5 Goal Evaluation	Goal setting questions answered:	_____	_____
	_____	_____	_____
STEP 6 Product	Complete, usable product plan:	_____	_____
	Shares what was learned:	_____	_____
	Quality of product:	_____	_____
	_____	_____	_____
STEP 7 Presentation	Creative/interesting:	_____	_____
	Organized:	_____	_____
	Teaches about topic:	_____	_____
	_____	_____	_____

Comments: _____

_____

_____

_____

Assessment

Assessment
IIM Conference Progress Log

Name: _____   Date seen: _____ _____ _____ _____

Topic: _____   Working on Step #: _____ _____ _____ _____

STEP 1 Topic

STEP 2 Goal Setting

STEP 3 Research

STEP 4 Organizing

STEP 5 Goal Evaluation

STEP 6 Product

Assessment

STEP 7 Presentation

 # Assessment
Debriefing for: *(Unit Name)*

Name(s): _____

Topic: _____ Date: _____

Using the 6 levels of Bloom's Taxonomy listed below, give information about the unit you have just completed.

Knowledge

List 5 facts you learned about your topic.

1. _____

2. _____

3. _____

4. _____

5. _____

Comprehension

Explain ONE of these facts in detail.

_____

_____

_____

_____

_____

_____

_____

Application

What did you learn that you could apply to a new situation?

_____

_____

_____

_____

_____

_____

_____

Assessment

Analysis

Compare your product with another one that you saw in your class.

_____

_____

_____

_____

_____

_____

_____

Synthesis

Imagine a way your product, another product, or the whole unit could have been different.

_____

_____

_____

_____

_____

_____

_____

Evaluation

Tell whether_____was a topic worth studying and why.

_____

_____

_____

_____

_____

_____

_____

Assessment

Assessment
IIM Teacher Observation Checklist

Class: _____

Unit: _____

Step(s): _____

Ratings

1 = Just Beginning   **3** = Made It

2 = Moving Up   **4** = Over the Top

BEHAVIORS OBSERVED

NAME OF STUDENT							COMMENTS

Assessment
Criteria List Rubric: *(Step or Skill)*

Name(s): _____

Topic: _____ Date: _____

Name of Peer Evaluator: _____

For the Teacher: *Create with class or assign criteria for quality work. If you decide to give a grade, use the total possible points to choose the range for letter grades.*

CRITERIA	STUDENT OR PEER	TEACHER	COMMENT
TOTAL			

Grading

A = _____   D = _____

B = _____   **Not**

C = _____   **Yet** = _____

Final Grade = _____

Ratings

1 = Just Beginning   **3** = Made It

2 = Moving Up   **4** = Over the Top

Assessment

Assessment
Moving from 1-4: *(Step or Skill)*

Name(s): _____

Topic: _____ Date: _____

For the Teacher: *Create with class or assign criteria and indicators for quality work. If you decide to give a grade, use the total possible points to choose the range for letter grades.*

1. Criterion: _____

Indicators: _____

_____

1 _____ 2 _____ 3 _____ 4

2. Criterion: _____

Indicators: _____

_____

1 _____ 2 _____ 3 _____ 4

3. Criterion: _____

Indicators: _____

_____

1 _____ 2 _____ 3 _____ 4

4. Criterion: _____

Indicators: _____

_____

1 _____ 2 _____ 3 _____ 4

Grading

A = _____   D = _____

B = _____   **Not**

C = _____   **Yet** = _____

Final Grade = _____

Ratings

1 = Just Beginning   **3** = Made It

2 = Moving Up   **4** = Over the Top

Assessment

Assessment
4 Square Rubric: *(Step or Skill)*

Name: _____ Topic: _____

For the Teacher: *List criteria and indicators for each rating number.*

Criterion:

1	2	3	4

Criterion:

1	2	3	4

Criterion:

1	2	3	4

Criterion:

1	2	3	4

Assessment

3 Skills Rubric: *(Step or Skill)*

Name(s): _____

Topic: _____ Date: _____

For the Teacher: *Using the number of indicators and total possible points, decide on a range for letter grades. Each indicator will receive a 1, 2, 3, or 4 to determine the scores. Total the scores for a final grade.*

STEP OR SKILL	RATING	INDICATOR
_____	_____	_____
	_____	_____
	_____	_____
	_____	_____
	_____	_____
	_____ = **Score**	
_____	_____	_____
	_____	_____
	_____	_____
	_____	_____
	_____	_____
	_____ = **Score**	
_____	_____	_____
	_____	_____
	_____	_____
	_____	_____
	_____	_____
	_____ = **Score**	
	_____ = **TOTAL SCORE**	

Grading

A = _____   D = _____

B = _____   **Not**

C = _____   **Yet** = _____

Final Grade = _____

Ratings

1 = Just Beginning   **3** = Made It

2 = Moving Up   **4** = Over the Top

Assessment
IIM Reflection: *(Step or Skill)*

Name(s): _____

Topic: _____ Date: _____

For the Teacher: List skills for ratings and reflections.

Skills:

	Always	Sometimes	Never
	_____	_____	_____
	_____	_____	_____
	_____	_____	_____
	_____	_____	_____
	_____	_____	_____

Something I/we did well:

_____

_____

_____

_____

_____

_____

_____

_____

Something I/we will work on next time to make this even better:

_____

_____

_____

_____

_____

_____

_____

IIM

Samples of Assessment Forms

OVERVIEW

These samples will show you how teachers have used the assessment forms for specific steps of IIM. You may adapt these forms to meet your needs or reproduce them as they are printed for your own classroom lessons.

Assessment
IIM Teacher Observation Checklist

Class: _____

Unit: _____

Step(s):   ALL SEVEN STEPS

BEHAVIORS OBSERVED

NAME OF STUDENT	STEP 1 Topic	STEP 2 Goal Setting	STEP 3 Research	STEP 4 Organizing	STEP 5 Goal Eval.	STEP 6 Product	STEP 7 Presentation	COMMENTS

Assessment

Assessment
Criteria List Rubric: *(Step or Skill)* **Presentation**

Name(s): _____

Topic: _____ Date: _____

Name of Peer Evaluator: _____

For the Teacher: Create with class or assign criteria for quality work. If you decide to give a grade, use the total possible points to choose the range for letter grades.

CRITERIA	STUDENT OR PEER	TEACHER	COMMENT
Shows knowledge of topic			
Organized			
Interesting			
Quality visuals			
Uses imagination & creativity			
Good voice tone			
Makes eye contact			
TOTAL			

Grading

A = 50 - 56   D = 30 - 36

B = 44 - 49   **Not**

C = 37 - 43   **Yet** = Below 30

Final Grade = _____

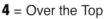

Ratings

1 = Just Beginning   3 = Made It

2 = Moving Up   4 = Over the Top

Assessment

 # Assessment
Criteria List Rubric: *(Step or Skill)*

Name(s): _____

Topic: _____ Date: _____

Name of Peer Evaluator: _____

For the Teacher: *Create with class or assign criteria for quality work. If you decide to give a grade, use the total possible points to choose the range for letter grades.*

CRITERIA	STUDENT OR PEER	TEACHER	COMMENT
Quantity of Notefacts:			
Quality of Notefacts			
Enough Information:			
Short:			
On Topic:			
Cites Pages:			
Paraphrased (not copied):			
Quality of Source Cards			
Information is accurate:			
Correct Format:			
Number of Resources:			
Types of Resources:			
TOTAL			

Grading

A = 72 - 80   D = 50 - 56

B = 64 - 71   **Not**

C = 57 - 63   **Yet** = Below 50

Final Grade = _____

Ratings

1 = Just Beginning   3 = Made It

2 = Moving Up   4 = Over the Top

Assessment

Assessment
Criteria List Rubric: *(Step or Skill)*

Interviews

Name(s): _____

Topic: _____   Date: _____

Name of Peer Evaluator: _____

For the Teacher: *Create with class or assign criteria for quality work. If you decide to give a grade, use the total possible points to choose the range for letter grades.*

CRITERIA	STUDENT OR PEER	TEACHER	COMMENT
Clear reason for interview:			
Researched background info:			
Questions			
Had icebreakers:			
Thorough:			
Some were open-ended:			
Prepared beforehand:			
Obtained needed information:			
Remained flexible to new ?s:			
Took good notes:			
Written thank-you:			
TOTAL			

Grading

A = _72 - 80_   D = _50 - 56_

B = _64 - 71_   **Not**

C = _57 - 63_   **Yet** = _Below 50_

Final Grade = _____

Ratings

1 = Just Beginning   **3** = Made It

2 = Moving Up   **4** = Over the Top

Assessment

Assessment
Moving from 1-4 Rubric: *(Step or Skill)*

Research

Name(s): _____

Topic: _____ Date: _____

For the Teacher: *Create with class of assign criteria and indicators for quality work. If you decide to give a grade, use the total possible points to choose the range for letter grades.*

1. Criterion: Quantity of Notefacts _____

    Indicators: At least 30 notefacts _____

    _____

    1 _____ 2 _____ 3 _____ 4

2. Criterion: Quality of Notefacts _____

    Indicators: Not copied, enough information, short, related to goal setting questions.

    _____

    1 _____ 2 _____ 3 _____ 4

3. Criterion: Number of resources _____

    Indicators: At least 3 _____

    _____

    1 _____ 2 _____ 3 _____ 4

4. Criterion: Types of resources _____

    Indicators: At least 3 _____

    _____

    1 _____ 2 _____ 3 _____ 4

Grading

A = 15 – 16   **D** = 9 – 10

B = 13 – 14   **Not**
                       Yet = Less than 9
C = 11 – 12

Final Grade = _____

Ratings

1 = Just Beginning   **3** = Made It

2 = Moving Up   **4** = Over the Top

Assessment
4 Square Rubric: *(Step or Skill)*

Big Book Page

Name: _____   Topic: _____

For the Teacher: List criteria and indicators for each rating number.

Criterion: Illustration - realistic

1	2	3	4
Little/no relationship to topic	Some use of color Accurate details	Effective use of color and details	Use of background details to enhance knowledge

Criterion: Writing mechanics - grammar, spelling, punctuation

1	2	3	4
5+ errors	3 - 4 errors	1 - 2 errors	No errors

Criterion: Research findings - facts on page

1	2	3	4
0 - 2	3 - 5	6 - 8	9 +

Criterion: Page layout - design elements

1	2	3	4
Random design	Some design plan	Effective use of measurement, spacing, text, and illustrations	Creative design enhances understanding

Assessment
3 Skills Rubric: *(Step or Skill)*

Group Product

Name(s): _____

Topic: _____   Date: _____

For the Teacher: *Using the number of indicators and total possible points, decide on a range for letter grades. Each indicator will receive a 1, 2, 3, or 4 to determine the scores. Total the scores for a final grade.*

STEP OR SKILL	RATING	INDICATOR
Research Process	_____	Goals were set and met
	_____	Notefacts were short and in own words
	_____	Notefacts correctly organized
	_____	Research organized neatly in folder
	_____	Participated and cooperated in group
	_____ = **Score**	
Report	_____	Interesting
	_____	Shows knowledge of topic
	_____	Written in own words
	_____	Neat, clear and well organized
	_____	Correct language and spelling
	_____ = **Score**	
Final Presentation	_____	Teaches something learned
	_____	Organized and attractive
	_____	Creative and interesting
	_____	Accurate use of vocabulary
	_____	Good voice tone & eye contact
	_____ = **Score**	
	_____ = **TOTAL SCORE**	

Grading

A = 55 - 60   D = 37 - 42

B = 49 - 54

C = 43 - 48   **Not Yet** = Less than 36

Final Grade = _____

Ratings

1 = Just Beginning   **3** = Made It

2 = Moving Up   **4** = Over the Top

Assessment

Assessment
IIM Reflection: *(Step or Skill)*

Oral Presentation

Name(s): _____

Topic: _____ Date: _____

For the Teacher: List skills for ratings and reflections.

Skills:

	Always	Sometimes	Never
____ We shared enough information.	____	____	____
____ We spoke loud enough to be heard.	____	____	____
____ We did not fidget.	____	____	____
____ We looked at the audience.	____	____	____
____ We were prepared.	____	____	____

Something I/we did well:

_____

_____

_____

_____

_____

_____

_____

Something I/we will work on next time to make this even better:

_____

_____

_____

_____

_____

_____

_____

Assessment

SECTION EIGHT

Teacher Resources

In this section, you will find background information about proven models and practices that form the foundation of IIM, and resources to help you implement the process. These include thinking skills and organizational teaching models that work well with our process, a listing of higher level thinking skills used by students while completing a research study, technology tips, a glossary of terms used in the manual, and a bibliography of resources.

CONTENTS - SECTION EIGHT

Teaching and Thinking Skills Models 215
Enrichment TRIAD Model 216
Research Strategies 217
Skills Often Used in Research 218
Glossary 219
Bibliography 221

Teacher Resources

Teaching and Thinking Skills Models

Talents Unlimited

Talents Unlimited is a thinking skills model created by Calvin Taylor and disseminated by the National Diffusion Network. The Academic Talent is the basis for the development of:

1. Productive Thinking
2. Forecasting
3. Communication
4. Planning
5. Decision Making

Bloom's Taxonomy

Bloom's Taxonomy is a hierarchy of thinking skills identified by Benjamin Bloom.
The six levels are:

1. Knowledge
2. Comprehension
3. Application
4. Analysis
5. Synthesis
6. Evaluation

Creative Problem Solving

Creative Problem Solving is a widely accepted system for solving problems.
Commonly used steps for this process include:

1. Mess Finding
2. Fact Finding
3. Problem Finding
4. Idea Finding
5. Solution Finding
6. Acceptance Finding

Cooperative Learning

Cooperative Learning, a concept spearheaded by Johnson & Johnson, is a grouping strategy that draws on student strengths and teaches mutual respect and responsibility.

Multiple Intelligences

This theory, developed by Howard Gardner, states that people possess "Multiple Intelligences" for learning, solving problems, and creating products.

1. Verbal–Linguistic Intelligence
2. Logical–Mathematical Intelligence
3. Musical–Rhythmic Intelligence
4. Visual–Spatial Intelligence
5. Bodily–Kinesthetic Intelligence
6. Interpersonal Intelligence
7. Intrapersonal Intelligence
8. Naturalist Intelligence

The Enrichment Triad Model

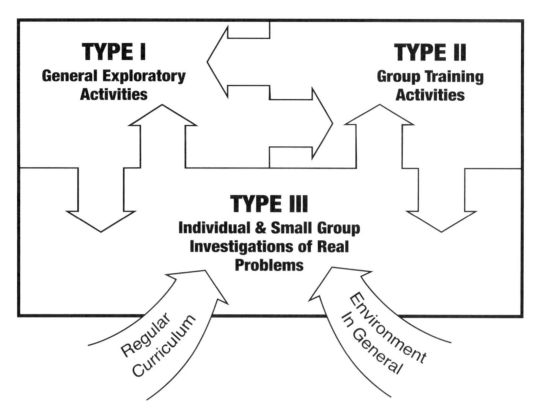

Type I Enrichment

Type I Enrichment consists of experiences and activities that are designed to bring the learner in touch with the kinds of topics or areas of study in which he or she may develop a sincere interest. Through involvement in Type I experiences, students will be in a better position to decide if they would like to do further research on a particular problem or area of interest.

Type II Enrichment

Type II Enrichment consists of materials, methods and instructional techniques that are concerned with the development of higher-level thinking and feeling processes. These processes include critical thinking, problem solving, inquiry training, divergent thinking, awareness development and creative or productive thinking. Type II activities are open-ended and allow students to escalate their thinking processes to the highest levels possible. Type II activities are also designed to introduce students to more advanced kinds of studies.

Type III Enrichment

Type III Enrichment consists of activities in which the student becomes an actual investigator of a real problem or topic by using appropriate methods of inquiry. The success of a Type III activity depends on the interest and task commitment of the individual student. Examples of intensive, long-range Type III activities include: the creation of a walking robot; the production of a dramatic marionette show which outlines the development of clowns from the thirteenth century to the present; a continuation of Tolkien's Lord of the Rings in the form of a novel; the writing and illustration of a Children's Christmas Book; etc.

Reprinted from *The Schoolwide Enrichment Model*, by Renzulli & Reis, with permission from Creative Learning Press, Inc.

Teacher Resources

Research Strategies

KWL is a method of condensing the parts of a research study on a matrix to show what students already **Know**, what they **Want** to find out, and what they have **Learned**.

KWL

Know	**W**ant	**L**earned
1. _____	1. _____	1. _____
2. _____	2. _____	2. _____
3. _____	3. _____	3. _____

The Big6 Skills Model of Information Problem-Solving is a model developed by Michael Eisenberg and Robert Berkowitz that defines a sequence of skills to carry out a research project.

1. Task Definition
2. Information Seeking Strategies
3. Location and Access
4. Use of Information
5. Synthesis
6. Evaluation

The I-Search Paper, developed by Ken Macrorie, is an end product of an I-Search, a research study based on the student's curiosity about a subject. The research phase must include an interview. By de-emphasizing rigid paper guidelines, the I-Search paper flows in a first person storytelling format reflecting the student's personality.

1. Introduction—What I knew already—Why I chose the topic
2. Body—The search process—Most important new learnings
3. Conclusion—Why this is significant to me
4. List of Sources

The Scientific Method is a way of researching used by scientists to test their theories.

1. Identify the problem
2. Gather data on the topic
3. Ask appropriate questions
4. Develop a hypothesis
5. Conduct experiments
6. Keep detailed records of methods and results
7. Report the experiments
8. Analyze the results
9. Develop a conclusion

4 Corners is an adaptation of Spencer Kagan's cooperative learning structure, Corners, which can be used successfully during many phases of the research process. Teams work cooperatively in each of the four corners of the room on an assigned task.

Skills Often Used in Research

1. Topic

Productive thinking

Concept mapping

Decision making

Identifying prior knowledge

Reviewing existing literature. . .

2. Goal Setting

Writing statement of purpose

Developing research question

Asking good focus questions

Setting individual goals for research study

Managing time. . .

3. Research

Using library

Choosing appropriate resources

Using different types of resources

Using correct format for bibliography

Interviewing, surveying, writing letters. . .

Accessing electronic information

Writing notefacts

Paraphrasing

Summarizing. . .

4. Organizing

Categorizing

Using graphic organizers

Outlining

Analyzing

Identifying areas needing more information

Formulating new ideas from data. . .

5. Goal Evaluation

Formulating open-ended questions

Evaluating quality of questions and answers

Evaluating quality of research data

Using test-taking strategies

Self-evaluating progress

Setting goals for next study. . .

6. Product

Productive thinking

Decision making

Synthesizing

Applying

Planning

Using product skills: graphic design, video taping, lettering. . .

Writing research report/paper. . .

7. Presentation

Choosing appropriate audience

Using presentation skills: public speaking, eye contact. . .

Communicating

Evaluating own/other presentations. . .

Glossary

Key Terms Used in this Manual.

Active research .... The part of an investigation in which there are no predetermined answers and data is accessible through action-based research (experiment, interview, survey...)

Analyze .... To identify the component parts of a whole

Assessment .... The use of both objective and subjective evaluation techniques to take stock of what has been learned in content and skills at any given point in the research process

Bibliography .... A list of writings on a given subject or by a given author

Working bibliography .... A record of all sources used in the research study

Works cited .... A complete list of all sources cited in a paper

Concept map .... A graphic organizer for collecting and organizing information

Data .... Facts or figures from which conclusions or interpretations may be drawn

Evaluation .... To take stock of what has been learned in content and skills at any given point in the research process by rating or grading

Objective evaluation .... Counting and rating the collected data and the 7 steps of the process

Subjective evaluation .... Personal judgment and interpretation of the data collected and of the 7 steps of the process

Goal Evaluation .... Accurate, measured appraisal of the goals set, data collected, the process used, and the skills developed during the research study

Graphic organizer .... Any of a number of visual representations that organize information into categories or sequences

Notefact .... A short, true piece of information extracted and recorded from a text source or from observations during action research

Essential notefacts .... Information selected from all notefacts which will become the evidence that supports the conclusions

Supplementary notefacts .... Information gathered during the research process that adds to the body of knowledge on the topic, but will not be used directly in the product and the presentation

Plagiarism .... Unacknowledged information, ideas, or writings appropriated and purposefully presented as one's own work including direct copying of source material without quotation marks and paraphrasing without an in-text citation (Lester and Lester, p.66)

Presearch .... A preliminary search of written information gathered by other researchers on one's topic of study (also called a review of the literature)

Research .... Focused investigation and experimentation about a topic to discover new facts

Research paper .... An end product of research in which a student defends a certain position or opinion by presenting new information, drawing conclusions, and attempting to persuade an audience.

Research report .... An end product of research in which a student summarizes the information gathered during the study

Resource .... Any book, article, interview, experiment, survey … used to gather the information for a research study

Source .... The specific place from which information has been gathered

Primary source .... A first-hand account of an event or an artifact created by the event where the author was present (newspaper, magazine article, dairy, collection, photograph, manuscript, archival document, political rally …)

Secondary source .... A source that seeks to describe, explain, and interpret an event after it has happened when the author was not present (book, article, media production, any historical source of reproduction…)

Synthesize .... To put research data together into a whole that expresses a new idea or creates a new product

Bibliography

Research Resources

Here is a list of resources used in the development of this manual. These books will give you more information about a variety of teaching strategies and research techniques.

Armstrong, Thomas. *Multiple Intelligences in the Classroom.* Alexandria: ASCD, 1994.

Baum, Susan, Robert K. Gable, and Karen List. *Chi Square Pie, Charts and Me.* Unionville: Trillium Press, 1987.

Baum, Susan M., Sally M. Reis, and Lori R. Maxfield. *Nurturing the Gifts and Talents of Primary Grade Students.* Mansfield Center: Creative Learning Press, Inc., 1998.

Burke, Kay. *The Mindful School: How to Assess Authentic Learning.* Palatine: IRI/Skylight Training and Publishing, Inc., 1994.

Eisenberg, M.B., and R.E. Berkowitz. *Information Problem-Solving: The Big Six Skills Approach to Library & Information Skills Instruction.* Norwood: Ablex Publishing, 1990.

Gardner, H. *Multiple Intelligences: The Theory in Practice.* New York: Basic Books, 1993.

Gibaldi, Joseph. *MLA Handbook for Writers of Research Papers.* New York: The Modern Language Association of America, 1999.

Kagan, Spencer. *Cooperative Learning.* San Clemente: Kagan Publishing.

Karnes, Frances A. and Kristin R. Stephens. *The Ultimate Guide for Student Product Development & Evaluation.* Waco: Prufrock Press, 2000.

Leiker, Kristal. *Effectively Incorporating Technology Projects in Your Classroom.* Bellevue: Bureau of Education & Research, 1997.

Lester, James D., Sr., and James D. Lester, Jr. *The Research Paper Handbook.* Glenview: Good Year Books, 1992.

Macrorie, Ken. *The I-Search Paper.* Portsmouth: Heinemann, 1988.

Renzulli, Joseph S., and Sally M. Reis. *The Schoolwide Enrichment Model: A How-To Guide for Educational Excellence.* Mansfield Center: Creative Learning Press, Inc., 1997.

Schack, Gina D., and Alane J. Starko. *Research Comes Alive! A Guidebook for Conducting Original Research with Middle and High School Students.* Mansfield Center: Creative Learning Press, Inc., 1998.

Schlichter, C.L. *Thinking Smart.* Mansfield Center: Creative Learning Press, Inc., 1993.

Starko, Alane J., and Gina D. Schack. *Looking for Data in All the Right Places.* Mansfield Center: Creative Learning Press, Inc., 1992.

Torp, Linda and Sara Sage. *Problems as Possibilities: Problem-Based Learning for K-16 Education.* Alexandria: ASCD, 2002.

Zorfass, Judith M. *Teaching Middle School Students to Be Active Researchers.* Alexandria: ASCD, 1998.

Teacher Resources
Here is a list of some of our favorite resources that will give you ideas to use for IIM.

Blandford, Elisabeth. *How to Write the Best Research Paper Ever!* Dayton: Pieces of Learning, 1998.

Bromley, Karen. *Graphic Organizers.* New York: Scholastic Professional Books, 1995.

Christenson, B.P. *Interview Research.* Buffalo: DOK, 1983.

Cooper, K. *Who Put the Cannon in the Courthouse Square.* New York: Walker and Company, 1985.

Deitch, JoAnn Weisman. *Get a Clue! An Introduction to Primary Resources.* Carlisle, MA: Discovery Enterprises, Ltd., 2001.

Fink, A., and J. Kosecoff. *How to Conduct Surveys: A Step-by-Step Guide.* New York: Sage, 1985.

Fredericks, Anthony D., and Isaac Asimov. *The Complete Science Fair Handbook.* Glenview: Good Year Books, 1990.

Heiligman, Deborah. *The New York Public Library Kid's Guide to Research.* Glenview: Good Year Books, 1998.

HyperStudio. Software. Cajon: Roger Wagner Publishing, Inc., 1997.

Inspiration. Software. Portland: Inspiration Software, Inc., 1993.

Johnson, Nancy. *Active Questioning: Questioning Still Makes The Difference.* Beaver Creek: Pieces of Learning, 1994.

Kid Pix. Software. Novato: Broderbund.

Bibliography *(cont.)*

McCubbin, Jacqueline. *101 Product Ideas*. Phoenix: Thinking Caps, Inc. 1980.

Nottage, Cindy, and Virginia Morse. *Let's Research Native Americans – Eastern Woodlands Tribes.* Kingston: Active Learning Systems, 2002.

Nottage, Cindy, and Virginia Morse. *Let's Research Native Americans – North American Tribes.* Kingston: Active Learning Systems, 2002.

Olenchak, R.R. *Digging Through Archaeology*. Mansfield Center: Creative Learning Press, Inc., 1989.

Philpott, Violet, and Mary Jean McNeil. *The KnowHow Book of Puppets*. London: Usborne Publishing Ltd., 1989.

Polette, Nancy. *Newbery Winners, Research, & the Internet*. Marion, IL: Pieces of Learning, 2000.

Polette, Nancy. *The Research Project Book*. O'Fallon: Book Lures, 1992.

PowerPoint. Software. Palo Alto: Microsoft, 1999.

Russell, Susan Jo, and Rebecca B. Corwin. *Statistics: The Shape of the Data*. Palo Alto: Dale Seymour, 1989.

Science Without Answers. Salt Lake City: The Wild Goose Company, 1989.

Simmons, Karen and Cindy Guinn. *A Bookbag of the Bag Ladies' Best*. Gainesville: Maupin House, 2000.

Tejada, Irene. *Brown Bag Ideas From Many Cultures*. Worcester: Davis Publications, Inc., 1993.

Terzian, A.M. *The Kids Multicultural Art Book*. Charlotte: Williamson Publishing, 1993.

Timeliner. Software. Watertown: Tom Snyder Productions, 1994.

Walker, Pam, and Elaine Wood. *Science Up to Standards*. Grand Rapids: Instructional Fair.
TS Dennison, 1998.

Weisman, D. *My Backyard History Book*. Boston: Little, Brown, Inc., 1975.

Web Sites

- **www.awesomelibrary.org** – gives information from selected databases. Just enter a search term or go directly to the database for academic and specialty area.

- **www.fno.org** – shares Jamie McKenzie's expertise on questioning and information literacy.

- **www.easybib.com** – The Free Automatic Bibliography & Citation Maker

Bibliography *(cont.)*

- **www.kn.pacbell.com/wired/fil** – helps teachers, students, and librarians develop Internet-based research activities. Student and teacher samples are included on the site.

- **www.noodletools.com** – a bibliography composer that formats your bibliography for you (small fee required).

- **www.plagiarism.org** – tracks on-line plagiarism, gives samples and tutorials.

- **www.teach-nology.com/web_tools** – many tools including one that generates 14 different types of rubrics and one that creates different graphic organizers. The home page also includes a place to locate good student search engines.

- **www.youth.net/nsrc/nsrc.html** – the National Student Research Center's recommendations on information, examples, and resources to help students conduct research.

- **www.7-12educators.about.com** – definition, activities, and ideas for preventing plagiarism.

We present a variety of IIM® workshops to train students and teachers in this effective method.

Check out our web site for more information
www.iimresearch.com

Call our office to talk directly to one of the authors
800-644-5059

E-mail us from the web site or at
info@iimresearch.com

ACTIVE LEARNING SYSTEMS WILL BE HAPPY
TO MAKE CONTACT WITH YOUR ADMINISTRATOR

We would also like to hear from you about The IIM Teacher Manual.
E-mail your ideas, suggestions, and/or experiences
as you help your students with strategies from our book.

IIM® Posters

These posters will reinforce and enhance the whole research process or specific skills you want students to master.

BULLETIN BOARD SET

This lively set includes cutouts of the 7 footsteps, a IIM sign, and Agent IIM in his detective garb. The students learn the vocabulary of research and keep track of their progress through their research study.

$9.95 each

7 STEPS TO SUCCESSFUL RESEARCH

Keep your students focused on the steps of the IIM research process with this colorful, concise presentation of the 7 steps. This poster features the skills of independent researchers.

$9.95 each

JUST SAY "NO" TO PLAGIARISM

This poster sends a powerful message to researchers of all ages: Good researchers don't copy! A definition of plagiarism and some tips on what to avoid reinforce the message.

$9.95 each

For information about books, materials, and training, contact Active Learning Systems at www.iimresearch.com or 800-644-5059

A Mini-Lesson Using

GOOD QUESTION CUBES*
to Promote Quality Questions

Teaching "How To" Skills

Curriculum Unit: *Your choice – this works with any content area.*

Step: *Goal Setting*

Date: *Any Day*

Skill: *Developing Quality Questions*

Class/Time: *30 minutes – any grade level*

Objectives:
Students will:

*   *Ask powerful questions to guide their study of the assigned curriculum.*
*   *Develop higher-level questions.*
*   *Make decisions regarding quality of questions generated.*

*Good Question Cubes

10 sets **$17⁹⁵**

Materials:

*   *Sets of* **Good Question Cubes.*** *(Red cube words:* How, Why, Who, Where, What/Which, When
    Blue cube words: Can, Is, Did, Might, Would, Will
    Green cube words: Predict, Analyze, Verify, Compare, Contrast, List*)*
*   **Muffle Mats*** *or other area to contain the tossed cubes.*

Procedure:

1. *Present your class with the focus of a curriculum area that needs to be researched.*

2. *Post 1-3* **Essential Questions** *that students must be able to answer from their research.* (Sample: "What are the common elements of war?")

3. *Model how to use the* **Good Question Cubes** *to develop goal setting questions to guide their research. Toss one red and one blue cube; read the pair of words; ask for questions related to the* **Essential Questions** *beginning with these words.* (Example for "Why Would": "Why would some men make better generals than others?" "Why would geography affect the outcome of a war?", etc.)

4. *Divide students into groups of 2-4. Have them record at least 3 questions for each toss of the cubes.*

5. *At the end of the session, have students choose the 3-5 most powerful questions whose answers will give information about your essential question (s).*

*Muffle Mat

10 for **$19⁹⁵**

Note:

Toss the green cube to promote higher-level question development.

THE PARENT GUIDE TO RAISING RESEARCHERS:
Book & CD *both for only* $24<u>95</u>!

This book and CD share with parents the successful IIM strate-   gies that have made Cindy and Virginia welcome in classrooms across the country as they model how to demystify the research process. Parents follow the stories of students *Allison* (Grade 3), *Larry* (Grade 6), and *Juanita* (Grade 10) as their research woes and successes unfold. Strategies in the **How to Help, Questions**, and **Do's and Don'ts** sections show parents how to give support without taking over the project as their children get from "Oh, No!" to "Oh, Yes" in research assignments.

KEY FEATURES

- Ideas on how to create a positive home environment for research
- Ways to have kids be "hands-on" and parents be "hands-off"
- Strategies for kids of all ages, abilities, and talents
- Support for each step of the process
- Power-packed bibliography for further support
- Reproducible pages for kids to use
- Fully interactive CD, "Rockin' Research", that permits students to do their research electronically

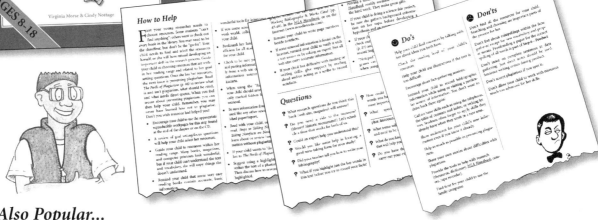

Also Popular...
Parent/Student Workshops to Enhance Your **IIM**® Teaching

In this unique workshop, Cindy and Virginia lead parents and their children through a typical assignment together, engaging them in action-oriented, interactive activities for each step of the research process. Parents learn techniques to support their children without taking over the assignment. Students share IIM techniques they already use in their own classrooms and learn strategies for places where they experience difficulty. A favorite with PTA's.

For information about books, materials, and training, contact Active Learning Systems at www.iimresearch.com or 800-644-5059.